Cross Country Skiing
The Norwegian Way

Second Edition --- Video Illustrated

Hanne Øverlier
with
Sindre Bergan

Total Health Publishing
Oslo, Norway

Copyright 2019

Table of Contents

Acknowledgments

We would like to thank the people who have contributed to this book.

First of all, thanks to Erik Olerud at Svea Skilag who prepared kilometers of ski trails for the models in this book. It was a big job to prepare the trails, and thanks to Svea Skilag for lending us the equipment, the driver and the tracks.

Svea Skilag has many good skiers and Erik pointed out two who would be good models for this book. The two promising athletes are Johan Gangsø and Marie Renée Gangsø, a brother and sister. Thank you both for skiing up the same hills and showing us the same techniques repeatedly. Erik also filmed for this book.

Thanks to Olov Belander, a former student at Norwegian University of Sports and a current friend. Thanks to my partner, Synnøve Solgård and our kids Ella and Even for modelling when mini-models were needed.

We would also like to thank Harald Bjerke from Swix for giving us the material for the chapters on waxing and equipment. Also thanks to Swix for letting us use pictures and content from their collections and products.

Preface

There is a saying that Norwegians are born with skis on their feet. I do remember a tough birth and it might be because of the skis they wore...

Skiing is however a big part of our lives. The kids are so excited about skiing that they have put their ski's on and practice their diagonal stride inside the house two years in a row, even when they watch TV or go to the toilet.

Norwegian skiing abilities probably correlate with the fact that we have snow, every winter and fairly long skiing seasons. We even go skiing in the summer, on wet snow from last winter (in the mountains). And if you do not make it to the mountains people roller-ski on the roads.

The winter's first snow is eagerly anticipated and almost sacred, every year. The first snow makes your tummy tingle, like being in love, and it builds as the snow builds up. The love affair is completed when there are mile after mile with tracks to ski on.

Our twins felt they grew up in a "pulk" (a sled carrying the kids which is harnessed to an adult, usually a parent). We live in the forest and were able to ski twice every day (maternity leave is long in Norway). The kids slept through beautiful sunshine and snowstorms, while we got more fit for each pound they added. I have never been as strong as I was the spring, they turned three years old. We had been pulling the pulk for miles while the kids alternately slept and giggled

The intersections and road-crossings are warning drivers about the trails and skiers crossing the roads.

This picture is from Valdres, a famous skiing area in Norway.

The last snow of the ski season is almost as sacred as the winter's first snow. It makes us ski on gravel and grass, because the season is about to come to an end. Most Norwegians have a pair of "gravel" skis that they use as the patches of dirt and grass wiggle up through the snow—searching for summer. Knowing that the next snow is six months away, we ski the gravel blemished snow. With summer we roller-ski the roads to keep our conditioning and improve our techniques.

Some people say that skiing for Norwegians is a religion, saying that it is better to go skiing and think of God than to go to church and think of skiing!

About this book

The chapters are written so that they can stand alone. You can therefore start wherever you want. If you are interested in equipment first, start there. If you want to understand the mechanics of skiing so that you can be more aware of why you should choose the equipment you want, start with the mechanics chapter. If you think that you want to learn the classic technique of traditional skiing, start there. But if you have had experience in ice skating or roller skating and think you can learn a skating technique easier, start with the skating chapter. Whichever approach you take, when you have read the whole book you will have a pretty good idea of the sport and the experience that is much more than a sport.

There are pictures on all techniques, and in relation to the pictures are videos that you can click on to see the technique more in detail. There are many videos in this book and we hope that they will give the reader good understanding of how to ski.

The links to use are in a table. In the digital version of the book you can click on the technique you would like to see—and it "magically" appears on your Internet connected device. But in the printed version you have to write the url address into your browser.

Links for e-book	Url- address for printed book
Press on the link (ctrl + click)	Write address into your web-browser
Diagonal stride uphill 1	https://vimeo.com/298341392/b11f48009c

CHAPTER 1
Introduction to Nordic Cross Country Skiing

When we think of cross country skiing — Nordic skiing — we think of Norway. The sparsely populated country of only five million people not only gave birth to the sport, but has dominated it in international competitions since they were first begun.

The saying that Norwegians are born with skis on their feet might be a bit of an exaggeration, but it is close to the truth. Infants are carried on the backs of their parents as they ski, or they are pulled in small sleds (pulks) behind one of the parents. It is not uncommon to see a father or a mother pulling an infant sled at the end of a 10-foot harness — then behind that sled is a small child's sled to be used by the child when the parents stop for a picnic along a trail.

The old-fashioned carrier/pulk is longer and lower, so that the kids are laying down in the carrier. In the more modern carriers, the kids can lie and also sit upright when they get bigger. The modern carriers can also be used as carriers behind bikes and as a trolley/carrier that you push, much like a stroller.

Throughout Norway there are machine-made trails which the skiers can follow for miles and miles. But the regal ranges of mountains and valleys beckon the intermediate skier to trek into the virgin snow which mantles the entire nation. In Oslo, the capital city, people ski on the streets and over the golf courses, but generally they find their ways to the top of the city and the great north woods (Nordmarka). Here at the last tram stop you can ski the prepared tracks, take off over the frozen lakes and pine-covered hills, or skate the advanced trails. And with the many miles of lighted trails, you can ski all night long if you so desire.

Whether you are skiing the open terrain under the canopy of blue sky or gray clouds, or passing beneath the crystal coated arches of the ice glazed pines or birches, the freedom of skis brings you closer to nature. It enthralls your soul with the frozen magnificence of winter's wonders.

Ah! But there's more to skiing than communing with nature. Cross country skiing is the finest aerobic exercise you can experience. It is better than running, swimming or cycling. It uses the muscles of the upper and lower body. It is a complete exercise and recognized by the leading fitness experts as the ultimate method for body conditioning.

Even disabled skiers at every age enjoy the freedom of the sport, whether skiing on a sled or a "walker" mounted on skis.

And as a hobby which the whole family can enjoy, there is no better activity than cross country skiing. Do you want competition? There are races. Do you want to ski, then shoot at targets? Try the biathlon. How about orienteering? In this activity you compete with compass and maps using your body and your wits to enjoy the day in the snow. Nordic skiing offers the complete spectrum of activities from recreation to competition.

So Nordic skiing — cross country skiing — can be whatever you want it to be — exercise, a union with nature, a source for competition or a vehicle to the ultimate in physical challenges. What do you want it to be for you? It is now "Your Sport."

About your skis

The skis are narrower than the Alpine (downhill) skis. The bottom of the skis will be smooth and slippery. These will allow the ski to slide through the snow with minimal friction. But in order to be able to push yourself through the snow, you must have a roughened area that will grip the snow. To achieve this roughened area, skiers use wax on the area just under the foot binding.

Depending on the temperature of the snow, different waxes are manufactured to be applied to this kick zone. Some skis are manufactured with a permanent roughened area in the kick zone. These are called waxless skis. These essential areas will be thoroughly discussed in a later chapter.

Your skis must be selected for your weight. When lying flat on the ground they will be flexed upward with the top of the arch under where your foot will be. If you are standing on both skis the arch will remain. But if you put all your weight on one foot, the middle of the ski will touch the ground so that the waxed area will come in contact with the snow. Consequently, lighter people will need more flexible skis, while heavier people will need stiffer skis. You will need an expert to fit you with cross country skis.

Balance: The Key to Skiing

We are giving you the basics in technique. Your technique will change with the snow conditions, the slope of the hill, your speed and your own feelings of competence. There is no "one way" to ski. You are an individual and you will ski as an individual. It won't be long before your friends will be able to spot you from a half mile away and say "there's old Christie" or "Well, look at James over there." Your style will be distinctive, and the real you will show through.

If your body is in good shape from aerobics, running or swimming, you may not need any extra physical conditioning. But if you have been a couch potato or a video nut you may want to prepare your body just a little. Look at the conditioning chapter early in your reading.

Balance is essential, because you should always be gliding on only one ski. That means you must have "one foot balance." We have given you some exercises for this. It is really much easier to spend five minutes a day for a few days increasing your balance ability than to try it first on the snow.

So, if you have the time and the inclination, spend a week or two getting ready before your first ski tour. If you don't have the time beforehand —just hit the snow and have a ball! (A snow ball?)

Also don't worry about equipment early on. Borrow it, or better yet, rent it. Just be sure that your hands stay warm. Your feet won't be a problem. They are usually toasty in their wool socks and leather boots.

Be ready to have fun! Five million Norwegians can't be wrong. The only thing on which they all agree is that "Skiing is Fun!"

CHAPTER 2
A little practice before you ski

Some people say that skiing is like walking — but it is really more like roller skating. You push and you glide. You transfer weight from one ski to the other. How can you get both push and glide from the same ski? That is done by proper waxing techniques which will be explained later.

For now it is enough to know that you push and glide. You push with a pole and your leg, while you glide on the other leg. Simple! It just takes a little practice.

When you ski, you glide — and gliding requires balance. That balance comes from a number of factors. The fluid in your inner ears is a major factor. As you move forward or backward, or side to side, the fluid in the three semicircular canals of the inner ear signals your brain to adjust your muscle tension in the hips, legs, back, arms, etc. So, the more you weave back and forth, the more signals your brain must send, and the more often your different muscles will have to contract to maintain your balance. As you become smoother, with less side-to-side motion in your skiing, there will be fewer signals for the brain to react to and fewer adjustments as well. So as your balance improves, your skiing improves — and as your skiing improves, your balance improves.

The eyes also play a part in your balance. Try closing one or both eyes and you will find it more difficult to balance. A common test that police give to suspected drunks is to have them close their eyes, then, with extended arms, try to touch their index fingers together. Not being able to see greatly reduces your ability to coordinate and balance.

Pressure on your feet or tension in your hips or legs also signals the body to make balance adjustments. As weight is shifted to one foot and you fall off balance outwardly, your brain signals the muscles on the inside of that leg to tense up, and you are pulled back to a balanced position. If you didn't quite get enough weight on that leg you would tend to fall inward, so the muscles on the outside of your lower leg and thigh tense up and pull you to a balanced position. This kind of balancing from one leg to the other occurs whenever we stand.

Balance is the shifting of your center of gravity over your base. The center of gravity is that point in your body which is the exact center of your weight. It is in the center of your hips. The exact location depends on where you carry the most weight. For this reason, women generally have a center of gravity slightly lower in their hips than do men. A person with heavier legs will have a lower center of gravity while a person with a heavier upper body will have a higher center of gravity.

Shorter people have centers of gravity closer to the ground so their balance should be easier. Taller people will have more problems because their center of gravity will be farther away from their base — their feet.

For example, the center of gravity of a "seesaw" or "teeter-totter" would be in the exact middle of the board. If two equally weighted children sit on opposite sides of the board, the center of gravity is maintained, and each can easily push off and ride up and down. If, however, a 50-pound child sits on one end and a 60-pound child on the other, the board will not move effectively because the center of gravity of the board will have moved toward the heavier child. So, to bring the center of gravity back to the middle of the board, the heavier child will have to move closer to the middle of the board until the center of gravity is again in the middle, and the children can easily move up and down with only a slight push.

Your center of gravity shifts right or left, forward or backward, as your body bends or your legs shift. If you bend at the waist 90 degrees, you will notice that your hips move backward and are no longer over the feet. But remember your center of gravity is over your feet; if it weren't, you would fall. So your balance must constantly adjust to the shifting center of gravity. And if that center of gravity moves outside of your base (your feet), you will fall — unless you can catch your balance by putting a pole down, by moving your arms to shift the center of gravity, or by shifting your weight on to the other ski.

To increase your balancing ability, it is best to practice balance exercises before you start to ski. However, if you have done a great deal of roller skating or ice skating, your balance may already be quite good, and you may be ready to hop on your new skis and hit the trail.

Training your balance without skis

If you are a beginner whose balance is questionable, you can practice at home without skis.

1) Stand on one leg, and balance as long as you can. Move to the other leg, and hold your balance as long as possible.

0) Hop sideways from one foot to the other. Hold your balance on one leg as long as you can, then hop to the other leg and hold your balance.

2) When you can do that easily, hop forward 6 to 10 inches on each hop. Then increase your hop distance and increase your balancing time on each foot.

3) Close your eyes and balance on both legs. Then do the same on the right leg, then the left leg.

You will need to get comfortable on your skis. Put them on. If the binding doesn't snap readily, check it to see that there is no snow or dirt in the binding or on your boot. If there is, clean it out and try again.

Now put your hand through the pole strap by bringing your hand upward through the strap. Bring your thumb and forefinger down on the pole grip. There should be little play in the strap because you want the strap to hold your hand comfortably close to the grip.

When you push on your pole to help propel you forward, there will be pressure on both your grip and on your strap. When you finish the push, you will relax your hand as you swing the pole forward. When you are ready to grip the pole again, the strap will have held the grip close to your hand. You will not keep a tight grip on your pole throughout your stride. You will grip as you push, then relax. If you kept a tight grip on the pole continuously, your forearms would be tense and might cramp. While skiing, you want your arms and legs to be as relaxed as possible.

Classical skiing without poles, balance training

Here are some drills to get used to being on skis and on the snow.

1) Try double poling and gliding. Extend your arms forward, plant the pole tips about even with your feet and not too wide. Then push with both arms. Feel the glide. Do it again. If you are skiing in tracks that have already been prepared, you will find it quite easy. Your balance will be easier to maintain because you will have a wider base of support.

2) Again, extend your arms in front of you, plant your poles about even with your feet. Now bend at the waist, use your abdominals to do the job and

then push back with your arms. You will feel even more power and will be able to glide farther.

3) While standing, lift one ski off the snow and balance. Then lift the other. See how long you can balance.

4) With your feet even, push back on the right pole and glide, then push on the left pole and glide. Do this until you feel comfortable and relaxed, swinging one arm forward as you push back with the other arm. Get a rhythm — right, glide, left, glide.

5) Without using your poles, jog on your skis. Take very short steps, and bounce along the trail. Bend your arms at the elbows, just as if you were jogging. The quick jogging steps will not require you to use much balance, but they will get your arms and legs coordinated with your right hand and left knee working together then your left hand and right knee. Don't even think about the coordination. If you can walk, your coordination will be fine. You just want to get the feeling of shifting your weight with your skis on.

When you feel comfortable with balancing on one leg while standing and balancing on both legs while moving with the double pole push and glide, you are ready to try classical skiing or skating. This is where you will find that either style is almost like roller skating or ice skating.

Here are three videos of skiing without poles:

Links for e-book	Url- address for printed book
Press on the link (ctrl + click)	**Write address into your web-browser**
Classical skiing without poles 1	https://vimeo.com/298229591/b82391e1a0
Classical skiing without poles 2	https://vimeo.com/298234265/ccb3b5202d
Skating without poles	https://vimeo.com/311047484/67f5212803

Skating without poles, weight-transfer and balance training

Should you fall before you have finished the book, just get your skis under you and stand up. You can't stand up with your skis to the side. But, of course, after you have completed the book you will never fall. You will have mastered the proper techniques and will have perfect balance. Once the snow realizes this it will never trip you up. (Pity the poor people who read other books. You'll see them falling everywhere!)

Intermediate Skills

Once you feel comfortable with the diagonal stride and the alternating arm coordination, as well as feeling the power of the arms and legs as you glide, you are ready for more intermediate skills. Be patient about moving to the intermediate level. It will probably take several sessions of practice before you feel comfortable.

Balance and weight shift is still a priority for the diagonal stride, and a skier should only be committed to one weighted ski at a time. Double poling is a very efficient technique to use with the diagonal stride of classic skiing. As you move into the intermediate level of skiing, you may want to consider double poling at times. The technique is aided by longer poles which allow force to be transmitted with a better angle. Longer poles and bending at the waist allow the skier to direct more force horizontally which results in more speed.

Here are two videos of the diagonal stride:

Links for e-book	Url- address for printed book
Press on the link (ctrl + click)	**Write address into your web-browser**
Diagonal stride uphill 1	https://vimeo.com/298341392/b11f48009c
Diagonal stride slight uphill 1	https://vimeo.com/298241932/b160222ebe

The Skills

1) Balancing on one leg.
2) Balancing alternately, one leg then the other.
3) Gliding on both skis.
4) Double poling — planting and pushing off both poles at the same time.
5) Single poling — alternately planting the right pole, then the left and pushing off the planted pole.
6) Jogging on skis.

CHAPTER 3
Diagonal striding and classic skiing

Learning the Traditional Method of Skiing

Classical skiing is the diagonal striding technique which fascinates us with the sport. It is a combination of walking and roller skating or ice skating. You push off on one leg and glide on the other. Of course, your arms will help a lot. Instead of just swinging them as in walking or skating, you push backward as you do in swimming. This makes classical skiing the best type of aerobic workout. It has the advantages of walking or running and swimming simultaneously. Add to this the fact that you are experiencing this activity in the great outdoors, and you have the ultimate sport — a combination of dynamic exercise with the aesthetic feeling of waltzing in a winter wonderland.

Getting the Feel of Gliding

It is the gliding that gives skiing that special feeling that you can't get while running. Let us review how to glide with the double pole push. With your weight on both skis, bring both arms forward. Plant the pole tips into the snow with the tips behind the hands. Push backward and downward with the arms. Then glide to a stop. Repeat this until you feel comfortable with the push back and glide.

Next, start with the same action, but as you push downward, bend at the waist letting your abdominal muscles work. Your power will now come from the abdominal muscles, the muscles of the upper sides of the back (latissimus dorsi) and the back of the upper arms (triceps). We will come back to this skill at the intermediate level.

Beginning to Ski

You develop the power by the push of one leg and the poling action of the opposite arm. The right leg and left arm work together, just like in walking. You may start your first diagonal striding by simply walking with short steps to get the feeling of walking on skis. If you are lucky enough to have a machine-prepared trail, it will be easy because the tracks keep your skis in line and at the proper distance apart. If you must go it alone on flat snow, you may find that your skis want to separate. Just put a little more tension on the muscles on the inside of your leg and you'll be fine.

Once you get the feeling of sliding on the snow, try to get a little glide. Push with the pole and leg, and glide on the forward ski. When you feel comfortable with a little glide, you will be ready to emphasize the push or "kick" with your power leg. Keep in mind, however, that if you don't use your kick to extend your glide, there is no reason for pushing! The glide is what it is all about.

One very important point to remember in all of your skiing is to bend your ankle. When your ankle bends, your knee bends. And when your knee bends, your hips bend. A major problem with beginning skiers is that they keep their legs too stiff.

The poles should be held loosely. The hand goes up through the pole strap then comes down on the handle. With this grip, the power of the arm swing can be transferred by a combination of pressures of the hand against the handle and the wrist against the strap.

The poles should be gripped loosely except during the power phase of

The skier should put her or his arm upward through the strap on the pole.

Don't grip it too tightly in order to avoid tension and fatigue in the hand and forearm.

the downward push. Gripping the pole too tightly can increase the tension and fatigue the hand and forearm.

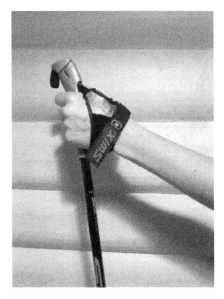

Modern polestraps

Modern polestraps are fitted more closely to the skier's hand.

The modern straps come in many different variants, and some have no straps – the glove is attached the pole.

The strapless poles are used by skiers doing biathlon, where they need to take their poles off and on for each shooting.

The Force Phase, or "kick" phase of the stride, occurs when weight is applied to the forward ski, and friction is developed under the center of the ski. At this point while your leg is moving backward, the ski should be motionless as the waxed area in the middle of the ski grips the snow and pushes against it. This phase will take about a third of a second. The beginning of the force phase of the stride occurs just as the gliding ski is pulled back and the foot is directly under the body. This happens when the rear ski is passing the front (gliding) ski.

Balance training without poles

If you have trouble coordinating your arms and legs, forget the poles for a while and just concentrate on pushing off with your foot. If you can find a slight downward incline, it will be much easier because each push will allow you a longer glide. All of your weight should be on the kicking ski. This allows you to press the waxed part of the ski into the snow and to get the maximum push. If your power leg slips backward when you push, you either do not have enough weight on it for your kick in other words; you kick too late. Another answer can be that the wax is not right for the snow. More about that in the chapter on waxing.

Even professional skiers train their balance and technique by skiing without poles. It is a great way of practicing weight transfer, where it is impossible to cheat by using your poles.

Classical skiing without poles, balance training

Here are three videos of skiing without poles:

Links for e-book	**Url- address for printed book**
Press on the link (ctrl + click)	**Write address into your web-browser**
Classical skiing without poles 1	https://vimeo.com/298229591/b82391e1a0
Classical skiing without poles 2	https://vimeo.com/298234265/ccb3b5202d
Skating without poles	https://vimeo.com/311047484/67f5212803

Skating without poles, weight-transfer and balance training

If you have trouble coordinating your arms and legs, forget the poles for a while and just concentrate on pushing off with your foot. If you can find a slight downward incline, it will be much easier because each push will allow you a longer glide. All of your weight should be on the kicking ski. This allows you to press the waxed part of the ski into the snow and to get the maximum

23

push. If your power leg slips backward when you push, you either do not have enough weight on it for your kick in other words; you kick too late. Another answer can be that the wax is not right for the snow. More about that in the chapter on waxing.

Intermediate Skills

Once you feel comfortable with the diagonal stride and the alternating arm coordination, as well as feeling the power of the arms and legs as you glide, you are ready for more intermediate skills. Be patient about moving to the intermediate level. It will probably take several sessions of practice before you feel comfortable.

Balance and weight shift is still a priority for the diagonal stride, and a skier should only be committed to one weighted ski at a time.

Double poling is a very efficient technique to use with the diagonal stride of classic skiing. As you move into the intermediate level of skiing, you may want to consider double poling at times. The technique is aided by longer poles which allow force to be transmitted with a better angle. Longer poles and bending at the waist allow the skier to direct more force horizontally which results in more speed.

Here are two videos of the diagonal stride:

Links for e-book	Url- address for printed book
Press on the link (ctrl + click)	Write address into your web-browser
Diagonal stride uphill	https://vimeo.com/298341392/b11f48009c
Diagonal stride slight uphill	https://vimeo.com/298241932/b160222ebe

Kicking Force:
Notice the kicking force with the fully extended left leg
and the reaching glide of the right leg.

The Pole Push is extremely important. Beginners often plant the pole too early for balance and push too little. The pole tip will be planted through as your abdominals and weight does the job. In the follow-through you use your arms more.

Plant the poles early, near the toes.

Plant the pole close to the toe of the boot

Double Poling

Double pole and glide. Keep the eyes forward, not down.

Here are some videos of double poling:

Links for e-book	Url- address for printed book
Press on the link (ctrl + click)	Write address into your web-browser
Double poling flat 1	https://vimeo.com/298347853/af5af03efc
Double poling slight	https://vimeo.com/298351781/2ab89a0b0c
phill 1	

Plant the poles near the toe of your boot or a bit farther back. Double poling is one of the fundamental techniques used in classic and skate skiing. As you apply your weight onto the poles you use our weight and abdominals in the first phase, the arms are more fixed. The movement is initiated from the hips when you have a slight lean forward. Then you transition to a follow-

As you get comfortable on your skis, work on a quicker pole plant and a long and powerful push. Plant your pole as soon as your hand reaches forward. Push down and backward with force. As you do this, your grip will change.

When your arm swings forward, you will "catch" the pole grip. You don't want to grip too hard, because it will be the strap which will be your major connection with the pole. If your grip is too tight, you will tense the muscles in your forearm and reduce the amount of relaxation which you want. So you will start with a firm (not tight) grip on the pole, but as the pole is pushed backward the grip is relaxed and more of the force of your swing is transmitted through your pole straps. When you have finished your push, your arm and pole will be in nearly a straight line. You can't keep the same grip on the pole as you did at the beginning of the action when the arm was at a nearly 90-degree angle to the pole.

To aid in the transmission of the power from the hand to the pole, some skiers will tighten the strap so that the pole grip stays closer to the hand. Others will finish the push with a tighter thumb-index finger grip on the pole. Whichever method you choose, keep in mind that at the end of your arm stroke, the pole will be closer to the horizontal position so more of your force is being transmitted effectively in the direction that you are skiing. But at the beginning of the arm stroke the pole is nearly vertical to the snow, so most of the power pushes upward and lifts the body.

The farther back the pole is pushed, the more horizontal power is generated and the longer your stroke the more efficient it is in developing power and speed, but the technique has changed in the last five years or so.

New and modern technique of double poling

For years, there has been a great development in skiing technique, we might talk about a revolution in classical technique. The impact of changes in double-poling is almost as revolutionary as the skating technique which was introduced in the mid-1980s by the American, Bill Koch. The last four to five years the skiers double-pole more in relation to their diagonal and double-pole with a kick. Some skiers have specialized at skiing without wax under their skis, or rather on skating skis, when in a classical race.

The skiers doing long-races (The Ski Classics) have contributed to this development, like the Swede Jerry Ahlin, his partner Laila Kveli and the Norwegian Aukland brothers. Already in 2008 Ahrlin stopped using kick-wax on his skis and in 2009 he won the prestigious Marcialonga. In the years to follow more and more skiers followed Ahrlin's lead and stopped putting ski-wax on their skis. In 2014 his partner Laila Kveli was the first woman to win the 90 km long Vasaloppet with no kick-wax.

Some more demanding and "hilly" races, even World Cup races, have been won without kickwax. In 2015 the Birkebeiner race in Norway, where you actually ski over the mountain, was won by Petter Eliassen on skis with no kick wax.

Why does double poling work so well?

First, it demands a lower oxygen uptake to double pole up hills than to go with diagonal striding. In the same way that you get a higher pulse rate while running with poles because you activate more of your muscles, the opposite happens in double-poling because you are using your upper body primarily. Thus, skiers who normally would have been left behind can do better with double-poling. It is especially in the semi-flat uphill runs that double-poling has proven to work particularly well.

In downhill runs, skis with no wax often do not have better glides than waxed skis. This is because the kick-wax area works well (is not in contact with the snow) as long as there is no more than half your weight on each ski. As soon as you get up and start to double-pole, the kick-wax will be in contact with the snow and create friction. So skiers will profit from not having kick wax on their skis. Another factor is that since double poling is only one technique, skiers do not need to spend time on changing techniques. In competition courses with many turns, skiers with no kick-wax will also benefit from gaining more power in the swing technique. This can also be an advantage in trails with demanding descents.

However, even if the skiers with no wax often climb the hills just as fast as those with kick-wax, they cannot keep the same speed on the top. And the snow on the course has to be hard in order for double poling to be better.

Norway's first doctoral thesis on double poling

Jørgen Danielsen is taking a doctoral.degree on double-poling and many of the athletes he researches competed in the Olympics in Pyeongchang. Danielsen says that many skiers will have a lot to gain from knowing more about when to double-pole and when to diagonal ski. Forget the long follow through and old-fashioned bowing over your skis.

With the new double-poling it is important to jump up with your legs and actively fall on the poles. The right technique is to stiffen large parts of the upper body and do fast movements forward. The whole body must be used to create a pressure on the poles which propel the body forward. In this way you use gravity to get ahead effectively, says Danielsen.

Double-poling technique is being studied extensively and is rapidly being improved. The number of skiers who win their races without kick wax has increased so much that the International Ski Federation (FIS) in the summer of 2017 introduced double-poling/banned zones in classic ski races in the World Cup. There is the fear that classical skiing could die out.

Danielsen has done research on double poling on the flats, slightly uphill and steep uphill - all at different intensities. He saw, among other things, the total effect in energy that was created, how the work was divided between different joints in the upper and lower body, and oxygen absorption. About 60 percent of the work in double poling at low intensity is in the upper body. With increasing intensity, and if it gets steeper, more and more of the work comes from the legs. The work in the legs then amounts to well over 50 per cent, says Danielsen. (https://gemini.no/2018/02/stak-deg-til-bedre-kondis-og-styrke/)

"This is the development, whether we like it or not," says Vegard Ulvang a merited Norwegian skier. "There is no doubt that classic cross-country skiing is in a transitional phase, and some may find it painful. But it is quick to double pole, and it is the development whether we like it or not."

"Double poling will pay off if one is strong. And double poling is easier to learn than diagonal. And then you don't have to wax your skis. For those who are growing up now, there will be only double poling and skating," said Anders Aukland, another top-flight skier.

Double poling-- the new technique

The new method of double poling is often called "sprinting."
like the videos in this book named "sprint".

Links for e-book	Url- address for printed book
Press on the link (ctrl + click)	**Write address into your web-browser**
Double poling sprint 1	https://vimeo.com/298353037/82c7b439d6
Double poling sprint 3	https://vimeo.com/298355455/ef54189ad5

Double poling on flat terrain or when sprinting

The lean forward is greater and the frequency is higher. The heels lift of the binding, the hips are higher, and your follow through is more with the whole upper body. The skier almost locks the arms and uses primarily the upper body (latissimus dorsi and triceps primarily), the abdominals and even the legs.

The pole plant should never be set behind the toe of the boot. This is to avoid the skis "slipping from the poles" so that you trigger all the power behind the body, where the muscles are weaker than the front and the torque becomes smaller. The force is going down through the rods and not into the air behind the body.

Stiffen your arms and shoulders just before planting the poles in the ground. This creates a stem that contributes to increased power in the double pole. Adjust the frequency to the terrain. If it is steep, the frequency must increase even if it is at the expense of the power of each double pole. If it is flat or downhill you can add more power to each double pole with a lower frequency.

Here are some more videos of double poling:

Doublepoling when it is flat

Links for e-book	**Url- address for printed book**
Press on the link (ctrl + click)	**Write address into your web-browser**
Double poling flat 2	https://vimeo.com/298349797/d53a5d0a07
Double poling sprint 2	https://vimeo.com/298354252/ec127af51a
Double poling slight uphill	https://vimeo.com/298351781/2ab89a0b0c

Double poling on a slight uphill

The fall forward is even greater than in easy/flat terrain. The body lean more on the poles and more use of the abs and weight.

Doublepoling uphill

Lets get back to the diagonal stride.

At the instant you plant your pole, your arm will be bent. Having a bent arm gives you a shorter radius from shoulder to hand. This makes it easier for your upper back and shoulder muscles to work effectively. It takes only one-quarter of the force to generate the same speed if your arm is bent at 90 degrees as it would if your arm were completely straight. However, your arm will be flexed only 30 to 45 degrees. (Racers will have a much greater angle at the elbow so that they can more forcefully extend their arms at the end of the poling action.)

Your initial force will come from your upper back (latissimus dorsi), rear shoulder (posterior deltoid) and back of the upper arm (triceps). If your arm were straight throughout the stroke, you would not be able to generate power from a large part of the triceps. But with the bent arm, you will generate more power during the final extension of your arm.

Stride Length is a major factor in skiing efficiency. Generally, the harder you push the longer you can glide. This relationship holds true at every level — from beginners to Olympians. Keep working on lengthening the stride by increasing your glide. Of late, skiers have increased their frequency to ski faster. It is not merely about gliding, but keeping the tempo high. For beginners it is important to focus on the feel of the glide and transfer of weight. If you aspire to be an Olympic champion you might work on finding the frequency that fit you. This differs a lot among the best skiers in the world, but are customized to the individual skier. The latest in classical skiing is the young man Johannes Klæbo from Norway, who on the steeper uphill "runs" on his skis. He lifts his skis as if he were running.

The first year he did this, the media, fellow skiers and spectators doubted his technique but we can see that skiers in the World Cup competition have tried to imitate his style.

Diagonal Stride: Be certain to glide on only one ski at a time.

The problem most often encountered here is the lack of one-legged balance. If you are having problems here, go back to the one-legged balance drills at home or on the snow. It may take a while to train the muscles on the inside and outside of your hips, thighs and ankles to correctly hold your body in the one-legged position. One-legged balance is critical to every phase of cross country skiing.

Here are some more videos of diagonal stride:

Links for e-ook	Url- address for printed book
Press on the link (ctrl + click)	**Write address into your web-browser**
Diagonal stride uphill 2	https://vimeo.com/298342984/eab1bf5c76
Diagonal stride uphill 3	https://vimeo.com/298344640/b66b3f0920
Diagonal stride slight uphill	https://vimeo.com/298244581/8c15b11e9d
Diagonal stride slight uphill	https://vimeo.com/298247136/f6e23a87d7
Diagonal stride front view S	https://vimeo.com/298236510/9e791b8cec

When you begin skiing, your strides will be short. Just concentrate on shifting your weight smoothly from one ski to the other. This will give you the feel of skiing. The balance will come if you are working on the one-legged balance exercises. As you learn to push off more forcefully, your gliding ski will be pushed forward more and your glide will be naturally increased. Classical skiing requires long leg strides and long arm swings.

Meanwhile, be sure that you keep your skis on the snow. Beginners often attempt to "walk" and lift the ski. This is not only inefficient, but it can ice up the ski bottoms. The snow on the bottom of the skis melts and then refreezes as it is exposed to the freezing air.

Concentrate on the glide. The push will generally take care of itself. Lean forward as if you are leaning into a stiff breeze. Your torso will be bent forward at about 45 degrees. Your chest will be nearly over your knee, and your ankle will be under your knee. Your thigh will be at an angle of 30 to 45 degrees from the vertical, and your weight will be on your heel. If you were to put weight on your toes, more of your waxed kicking area would come in contact with the snow and slow you down. Naturally, you don't want your kick wax hitting the snow when you are gliding.

Keep head bobbing to a minimum. Some up-and-down movement is unavoidable but excessive vertical movement is counterproductive.

Diagonal stride: kick with the weight on your heel

Double pole with a kick

When it is too flat or fast to diagonal ski and too steep to double-pole, it is time to use a technique called double pole with a kick.

To pole with a kick, kick first, then immediately double pole, then glide on both skis. The kicking leg will recover as you begin your double pole movement backward. Be sure to let your body weight provide most of the pole power. It is the bending at the waist, not the push back of the arms, which should provide most of the power. You will first bend powerfully at the waist, using your abdominal muscles, then extend your arms backward.

Here are some videos on double poling with kick:

Links for e-book	**Url- address for printed book**
Press on the link (ctrl + click)	**Write address into your web-browser**
Double poling with kick 1	https://vimeo.com/298356851/36ed547093
Double poling with kick 2	https://vimeo.com/298358056/8140aef1b4
Double poling with kick 3	https://vimeo.com/298359396/e753b21947
Double poling with kick 4	https://vimeo.com/298360613/d343261a56

Changing from diagonal striding to the double pole and kick is a skill that should be mastered. Terrain conditions or fatigue may require a change of poling for maximum efficiency. To change from diagonal striding, you can leave one arm forward while the other arm recovers and moves forward. Now with both arms forward you are ready for a double poling thrust. Another method is to leave one arm back until the other arm completes its push, then bring both arms forward together. Try both methods to see which is more comfortable for you.

To change from double poling to single poling/diagonal striding, you can leave one arm back when the double poling thrust is completed. Then move one arm forward as the opposite leg moves forward, and you are diagonal striding again.

Poles are placed right by the toe of the shoe, the fall forward is marked with blue lines

Ski your own way after you have mastered the basic techniques. Some people have powerful arms and will emphasize the arm push. Swimmers and gymnasts are likely to have such power. Others use their kick as the major propulsive force. Runners and those whose former sports interests included running, such as basketball or football, will often rely heavily on the kick. Old injuries may play a part in how you ski. Ankle, knee or back injuries may affect your ability to flex those joints. Also, injuries may reduce your ability to push backward.

Kick down (left foot) when arms passes the hip on the way forward

Force or Push Off
1) Hips over your feet.
2) Upper body leans slightly forward.
3) Feet parallel, with both feet under your body.
4) Legs are flexed at the knee.
5) Lift one arm forward; plant the pole with the tip near your toes.
6) Push back with the arm while kicking back with the opposite leg.

Gliding
1) Upper body leans forward.
2) Eyes look ahead, not down at the skis.
3) Weight shifts completely from the kicking ski to the other ski — the gliding ski.
4) The arm opposite the gliding ski swing s forward.

Common Problems
1) Using poles for balance — To correct this, keep them out to the side of the body, instead of pushing with them. Drop the poles and let your arms swing naturally as if you were walking or running.

2) Poor coordination of arms and legs — Drop the poles and let the arms work naturally. Or, drop the poles and jog on your skis, taking short, quick steps. Let your arms work as they would if you were jogging.

3) No glide because the weight isn't transferred to the gliding ski since the weight is kept on both skis for better balance — Stop and lift one leg and balance, then lift the other leg and balance. Begin again, emphasizing the one-legged balance as you glide.

4) Your kicking ski slips — Stand more upright with the hips forward and the torso forward. Are you transferring all of your weight to the push off ski? Check your wax. It may be the wrong wax or it may not be thick enough. (See Chapter 10.)

5) Your skis hit the snow early and make a slapping sound — Your upper body is not far enough forward so that your trailing ski hits the snow before your foot is under your hips.

Beginner
1) Find a flat area then walk on the skis without poles. Swing the arms straight forward and backward. The hands should not cross over the skis.
2) Jog with very short steps without poles.

3) Push with both poles and glide.
4) Try all of the above on a slight downward slope so that gliding is easier.

Intermediate

If your double poling is not as effective as it might be, it may be wise to:

1) Check to see that you are not squatting (bending your knees too much) when you bend at the waist.
2) Check also to see that your upper body is bent nearly 90 degrees at the waist. It is the weight of the upper body, not the arm strength, which is the key to arm power.
3) Accent the push backward with the arms as the final thrust of the movement.

CHAPTER 4
Going Up Hills

Going up hills is an essential part of cross-country skiing. The techniques are quite simple to learn. The problem is that it uses much more energy than going downhill. As a beginner, you may be led to believe that the course is 98 percent uphill with the two percent downhill being in a straight drop. Of course, that isn't quite true — except in Norway! The usual downhill run is only a 45-degree slope! Well, not quite.

As with every other aspect of Nordic skiing, there are beginner, intermediate, and advanced techniques. We will look at the beginner and intermediate techniques in this chapter while the advanced methods are included in the chapter on skating.

Beginner Techniques

Both the side step and the herringbone, or as the Norwegians call it, the "fish bone," are beginner techniques which all skiers will use sometimes. The conditions which determine when they will be used by the more advanced skiers are the degree of the slope of the hill or the condition of the snow, such as the amount of ice.

You do the **side step** by getting your skis across the "fall line." That is, get your skis exactly perpendicular to the slope of the hill. Keep your body erect, your head up and your poles outside of your skis. From this position bend your knees slightly and move them toward the slope of the hill. As your knees move toward the hill, your ankles, boots and skis will also tilt toward the hill.

The movement of the boot pushes the uphill edge of the ski into the snow and lifts the downhill edge of the ski. The ski is now "edged" into the snow so that it bites into the snow. The steeper the angle of the slope of the hills, the more "edge" you will need to keep the skis from sliding down the hill. Take small steps at first to get the feel of the edged ski. Lift the uphill ski 6 to 10 inches up the fall line, then bring the other ski up to it. Keep repeating this movement as you climb the hill.

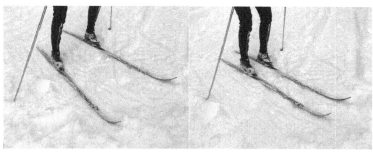

Edging the skies into the snow

39

Side step

Use your poles for balance, especially the downhill pole which can be used for an extra push off as the uphill ski is moved up the hill. Also use that pole to stabilize your body as your downhill ski is brought up to the higher ski. Keep your body erect, your head up and your poles outside of your skis.

If your skis begin to slip sideways, you don't have enough edge into the hill. Just bend the knees more into the slope. If your ski tips or tails begin to slide downward, you have moved away from the fall line. Find the fall line again. If your tips were slipping downward, they are closer to the fall line so move toward them. If your tails were slipping, move them up the hill and move toward them.

The Herringbone

The **herringbone** obviously gets its name from the type of tracks it leaves in the snow. They look like the bones of a fish seen from behind the backbone — sort of a gourmet's eye view after you have boned the trout

Note: Very few hills have a perfectly consistent fall line. Every bump of snow, every mogul, and every rock can change the fall line.

While beginners may use this technique on many hills, the advanced skiers use it only on the steepest hills or on very slippery ice. Since the side-stepping technique is used for climbing any kind of hill, you should learn to be comfortable with it early in your career. Learn to do it with your left side to the hill and with your right side toward the hill.

From facing the hills sideways we now move to facing the hills straight on. We introduce the herringbone. It is easiest to start doing the herringbone on flat land. Move your ski tips outward while keeping the tails close together. Your skis will now form a "V." Walk forward a few steps while using the poles to help to push you.

Now start up the hill.

Keep the same V position of the skis with your poles outside of the skis. As you begin to go up the hill, bring your knees and ankles inward to edge the inside of the ski that is on the snow. This will prevent you from going backward. There is nothing magic about the V position of the skis if they are flat on the snow. You will still slide backward unless they are edged.

The advanced skiers will almost jump on each step when they do the Herringbone on a steep hill. When the hill is less steep, they go for a more diagonal version of Herringbone, where the skis are more parallel in the snow (directed upwards)

The Herringbone front

Stand upright and keep your head up. This will help to keep your weight centered over your boots. Bending forward shifts your weight back toward your heels. Take reasonably large steps. The shallower the slope, the longer the steps you can take. Use your poles just as if you are walking, with the right arm swinging forward while the left leg moves up the hill. Be sure to plant the pole well behind your hands so that it is angled backward. This way it can be used effectively to push.

41

If you start to slip backward, widen the V of your skis and edge in the ski on which you have your weight. Do that by bringing the knee inward on the ski which you are edging. Then use your poles, exerting more push on each step.

Here are some videos of Herringbone:

Links for e-book	Url- address for printed book
Press on the link (ctrl + click)	**Write address into your web-browser**
The Herringbone steep hill	https://vimeo.com/298363391/34f4cc2368
The Herringbone steep hill	https://vimeo.com/299271922/068440361d
The Herringbone steep hill	https://vimeo.com/299275913/912a52046d
The Herringbone 1	https://vimeo.com/299279997/f9198b74ce
The Herringbone 2	https://vimeo.com/299288417/7bfd83a648
Oops, something went wrong...	https://vimeo.com/298361985/d564b2c6af

The videos "The Herringbone 1 and 2" show that if the hill is not so steep, the V will be narrower and the Herringbone will look more like a diagonal stride.

Poling becomes quicker and stronger as you go uphill. The steeper the hill and the less the skill, the more strides will be taken per minute. Consequently, the more frequent will be your pole plants. The poles will also be planted farther back to propel you up the hill. Since quicker poling action will be taken, the arms will be bent more. The shorter the radius from your shoulder to your hand, the more power you can generate from your shoulder and arm muscles. So, the steeper the hill, the greater the elbow bend and the quicker the poling action.

When the slope of the hill is more flat, the V of the skis will be tighter and the skis can be kept nearly in parallel.

The Herringbone in series

Still greater force can be exerted if you use your abdominal muscles, along with gravity, to force the poles downward. Your shoulder muscles will merely hold your poles steady while the abdominals start the downward movement of the poles. Then, when the abdominals have exerted their force, the shoulder muscles and the triceps continue to push the poles backward.

Sometimes it is hard to get the skis and the poles in the right order. If you look at the videos there is one video, when the Herringbone went wrong: "Oops, something went wrong".

The Diagonal Stride and Herringbone Step

When you are able to approach the hill with more speed, you can continue your diagonal striding up the hill. If you can do this, it is much easier than using the herringbone step.

A slight slope of the hill gives a tight V angle for the skies

To stride up the hill, you must aggressively transfer all of your weight to the force ski, the kicking ski. You want to be able to get the wax pocket, or the kicking area of the ski, completely into the snow so that you can get the maximum amount of friction possible. You will also want to lean with your hips forward. You must be certain that you are not leaning too far forward or your hips will be pushed too far back in order to maintain your balance. If your hips are too far back, or you are bent too much forward your skis will slip. Keep your hips forward.

Using the diagonal stride

Naturally, your poling will also be harder than when skiing the flats. You will not push as far back as you do when skiing on a level trail, because your arms and legs will be moving quicker to keep your speed up the hill. When we discuss skating up hills in Chapter 7, you will have other options for moving up hills effectively.

Here are some more videos of diagonal stride:

Links for e-book	Url- address for printed book
Press on the link (ctrl + click)	**Write address into your web-browser**
Diagonal stride uphill 2	https://vimeo.com/298342984/eab1bf5c76
Diagonal stride front view H	https://vimeo.com/298237631/b938daa61d

Checklist

1) Keep your gliding knee over your foot. If your gliding foot gets ahead of your knee, you will lose power because your hips will be forced backward.

2) Keep the angle at your ankle, about 90 degrees. If the knee gets too far ahead of your foot, your hips will tend to move up and down, and you will lose power.

3) Reach forward with the gliding hip to increase your glide uphill.

CHAPTER 5
Going Down Hills

You can be certain that you will be doing some downhill skiing on your tour unless the course is perfectly flat. For every hill you go up, there is a hill to go down. If you were to ski in an international race, you would be assured that at least a third of the course would be downhill.

Downhill skiing gives you the feeling of flying, with the wind whipping through your hair and bathing your face. If you are a recreational skier, you can use this downhill run for resting, or you can enjoy the rush of a "shush" for its excitement. If you are a racer you will want to add even more speed and pick up more time against your competition. But let's start with the most basic skills.

Side Slipping

A very important skill to learn is the side slip. To do this, stand on a hill with your skis across the fall line. Move your knees and ankles toward the downhill side. The skis should begin to slip downhill. To stop, move the knees and ankles inward toward the uphill side.

Once comfortable with side slipping and stopping at a right angle to the skis, try side slipping forward and backward. To side slip in the forward direction, lean your weight forward so that more weight is on the toes, move the knees and ankles toward the direction you want to move, and flatten your skis on the snow. To side slip backward, put your weight on your heels, slip into a position in which your heels point in the direction you want to move, and fl at ten the skis on the snow.

The sideslip technique should be mastered, because it is essential for very steep inclines and for icy conditions. It will give the beginner great confidence in any type of terrain. Even the expert may need to side slip forward and backward when moving down a treacherous slope which is either steep or icy, or both. If you don't learn to side slip, you may have to spend the rest of the winter on some steep icy crevasse —just you and the polar bears.

The Wedge (Snow Plow)
The most **To execute the wedge:**

1) With the legs fairly straight, push the heels outward and the toes inward. The front tips of the skis can be as much as 12 inches (30 cm) apart.

2) The upper body bends slightly forward at the hips.

3) More weight is put on the heels to allow for pushing the heels outward to control the tails of the skis.

4) The poles can be tucked under the arms. important technique to learn for beginners is the wedge.

The wedge is used at all levels of skiing

To control the speed or to stop, bring the knees inward. This edges the skis and creates more friction. Simultaneously, increase the angles of the skis by pushing the tails outward or by bringing the tips inward.

To move faster down the hill, move the knees outward to flatten the skis on the snow.

The Half Wedge

The half wedge is handy when you are skiing in tracks and going downhill. If you want to slow down, just bring one ski out of the track and put it into the wedge position. The ski in the track will keep you in the proper path. The wedged ski will allow you to slow as much as you want by widening it or by edging it.

Edging the wedge

The outside edges of the skies are up

and

the inside edges of the skies «applies the breaks» so you can stop.

48

The half wedge

Following the Fall Line

Skiing straight down the hill is really quite simple — especially in tracks. Just lean your body a bit forward so that your knees are forward of your ankles. Increasing the bend at the knees lowers your center of gravity (the spot where your weight is concentrated — in the middle of your hips) and makes you more stable. Have your weight equally balanced on both skis.

Tuck Position

As you ski down the hill in this "tuck" position, try to keep your center of gravity (in your hips) parallel to the snow. That is, try to keep your hips the same distance from the general slope of the hill all the time. You will be skiing with your knees slightly bent. If you come to a bump, bend your knees more to absorb the shock. If there is a little dip, extend your legs so that your hips stay as close to parallel with the angle of the hill as is possible. It is essential to stay relaxed and flexible.

If you really want to go fast, make yourself into an egg — that's a yolk! You will have to bend forward to decrease wind resistance. The ultimate speed position is what we call the "egg" shape which is very aerodynamic.

Egg Position

Skiing Across the Fall Line (Traversing)

In skiing across the mountain, you will need a slightly different technique. Obviously one ski will be higher on the hill than the other. The uphill ski will be slightly advanced of the downhill ski. This will happen naturally if you turn your body slightly down the hill. Having one leg forward will give you better balance.

Most of your weight will be on the trailing downhill ski. Try to keep the skis flat on the snow without edging them. This is done by moving the ankles slightly outward toward the downhill side. If, however, the snow is icy or you are going fast, you may need to edge the skis by bringing the knees and ankles inward toward the top of the hill.

Skiing across the fall line

The Traversing Side Slip

You may want to move farther down the hill when traversing. This can be accomplished by adding a side slip to your forward traversing direction. During your traverse, move your knees more outward and point the toes more downhill than when you are merely traversing. Flatten the skis on the snow and begin sliding at a sharper angle downhill.

If you begin to go too fast, just bring your knees closer to the upward slope of the hill and your skis will edge. If you want to go still slower, turn up the hill.

Skiing Downhill

For most people, skiing downhill is the most exciting aspect of skiing. In order to make it the most enjoyable, you must practice, practice, practice. And your major achievement must be balance, balance, balance. A key ingredient in your ability to ski downhill fast is how much courage you have. This is just as true for world class racers as it is for the beginner skier.

If you are nervous or scared, you will be tense. Your balance will be affected because all of your muscles are tense — not only those used to hold your balance. Yet some people have this natural courage (insanity?). Teenage boys often are quite ready to go full speed without knowing where they are going. Speed without direction, in life or on the slopes, is not intelligent.

If you find that you're a bit apprehensive about a downhill run, start with the snow plow or use a half wedge with one ski in the track and the other wedging and slowing you. Once near the bottom of the slope put both skis in the track and ride it out. Work to go just a little faster each time. Start your parallel skiing just a bit higher on the hill and increase your confidence.

Bend forward and think of being aggressive. The typical beginner carries the weight back, as if digging in with the heels. This won't work. Bend the knees slightly, bend forward at the hips and hold your hands in front of

51

you. This should get your weight forward and provide you with the aggressive feeling and control that you want.

Going Faster

To zoom down the hill, you have to reduce the air resistance against your body. The faster you go, the greater the air resistance. To decrease wind resistance and ski faster, get into a tuck position. Bend the knees 90 degrees or more. Bring your chest down to your thighs. Keep your weight forward. Tuck your poles under your arm pits. The angle at the elbow will be 90 degrees. So make yourself into an egg — and fly!

One of the world's top three skiers does not go all the way down to the "egg" position. He keeps his legs almost straight. The reason, he says, is that while the egg position is more effective, it tires his thigh muscles, and he must be ready to climb the next hill. He sacrifices some downhill speed so that he can rest for the uphill climb. His view is definitely in the minority, but it may be worth thinking about.

As a recreational skier, you can control where you ski and how fast you will take the hills. But racers have to take steep downhills, as steep as 40 degrees, at top speeds, and sometimes for several minutes. At the 1995 World Championships in Thunder Bay, Ontario, Canada, there was a downhill run of more than two minutes.

If you do Alpine skiing, your Alpine skills will help you on your downhill runs. In Norway, we often bring in the Alpine downhill coaches to assist our Nordic skiers in their downhill techniques. After all, skiing is skiing!

Skiing Different Types of Snow

Powder is the ultimate, but it may be unforgiving. If you are lucky enough to get powder on a hill, or if you have decided to go far off the beaten track, you can have one of the greatest experience of your life.

Keep your weight equally distributed when skiing downhill in powder. Make your turns as fast or as slow as you like, but finish every turn. If you head straight down the hill, you may be in a little trouble and may have to brake yourself with a "head plant" in the deep snow. So make your full turn to control your speed. The powder helps to slow you down, but it won't do it all.

If you haven't done it before, find a slight slope with new powder. Walk up the hill a little way, and then ski straight down. Put more weight on the left ski, then the right. See how your balance feels. You will find that even distribution is best. After a few straight runs to get the feel, try a straight run while you are bending your knees. Move your hips up and down.

Once you feel comfortable with your straight shots down the hill, you are ready to try a Telemark or a parallel turn. (See Chapter 6.) Plant your pole in the direction you want to turn. Telemarkers will move the opposite ski forward and the near ski back while they carve the turn. Parallel skiers will emphasize the weight on the outside ski but can edge both skis in making the turn.

Checklist

1) Bend forward with your weight slightly on your toes.

2) Get into a crouch position or an "egg" position if you want to go faster.

3) Keep your weight on both skis.

4) Be ready to absorb the bumps with your legs by keeping your knees bent.

CHAPTER 6
Stopping and Turning

Stopping and turning are related movements. The simplest type of stop and turn develops from the wedge position. You simply slide the skis out at the tails, edge the inside edges, and you will slow and stop. To turn, slide one ski out at the tail and edge it, and you will turn in the direction that it is pointing. If you are going too fast down a hill, you merely turn up the hill and you will stop.

Skills Needed

- Sliding a ski out and in.
- Edging on the inside of each ski.
- Steering the skis with the lower body.
- Stepping out with one ski while the weight is on the other one. To

slide the ski: Put your weight on one ski and slide the other out with the base of the ski flat on the snow.

You can practice this at home on a rug or wait until you are on the snow. It is just a matter of balance. First, slide one ski out, then bring the skis together. Then slide the other ski out and bring the skis together. When you can do this comfortably, slide into a half wedge position by moving just the tail of one ski outward, keeping the tips of the two skis together.

Once you are on the snow, repeat the drills. When you feel comfortable with the one-legged sliding, slide both tails outward and make a full wedge position. Do this several times. After you have mastered sliding to the wedge, simply wedge your skis and bring your knees together. This will edge the inside edges of your skis, and you will be in the stopping wedge posture, commonly called the "snow plow."

To *edge* the skis: Move the knee inward while keeping the ankle stiff. This pulls the outside of the ski up, and your inside edge is "edged" into the snow. You may use this technique when traversing across a hill if your skis begin to slip downhill. You will also use it in some turns. It is also essential in the wedge stop or snow plow.

To *steer* the skis: Turn the whole leg in the direction that you want the ski to go. This is actually done in the hips where the thigh bone is turned or "rotated" around its long axis. But the key is the connection of the foot to the ski. If the foot moves, the ski will move.

To *step:* Put all of your weight on one ski while you lift and move the other outward.

To *stop in a prepared trail:* Lift one ski out of the track and put it into a wedge position. You can lift the ski and put it in that position, or you can lift it out of the track, put it on the snow, then slide it to the wedge position. Once it is wedged, you angle your knee and ankle inward so that the ski "edges" then you put more weight on that ski to increase the edging effect and to push against the snow to slow or stop your momentum.

To *stop out of the trail while coming down a hill:* Slide both skis out with the toes in and the tails out. The wider the angle of tail to tip, the greater your potential stopping power. Once they are in the proper position, bring the knees and ankles inward to create edges. This edging pushes against the loose snow and slows you down.

Another way to stop if you are on an open hill is to turn up into the hill. Let the skis slide as you steer them toward the uphill direction, then edge the lower ski as you continue to steer away from the fall line (the line directly down the hill).

The Wedge

The wedge

Find a slight incline, such as at the bottom of a hill. Climb up and slide down. Try it first with the skis flat on the snow. Move the tails in and out, getting the feel of sliding into the wedge then back into the parallel position. Now move a little higher on the hill and start down. As you slide your skis out into the wedge, lower your hips and bring the knees and ankles inward for edging. If you don't stop, try a wider wedge position, with the heels farther out. Next try greater edging by bending the ankle and the knee even more.

The wedge turn is generally used by beginners and by others when the snow is hard or packed. From the narrow wedge position with your skis sliding down the hill, steer both skis with your knees and feet.

The wedge turn

The wedge turn

For a sharper turn, you can put more weight on the ski that you want to be the outside ski in your turn. Edge the ski by bringing the knee and ankle closer to the middle of the wedge as you lean outward on that ski. In other words, put your weight on the ski that is pointing in the direction that you want to go. So, put your weight on the right ski if you want to turn left, or the left ski if you want to turn right. Keep your hands low and the tips of the poles pointed backward. And presto, you're there. Then you can make one turn in the other direction. This is called "linking" turns. When you feel comfortable with this activity, move farther up the hill and link some more exaggerated turns. As your turns become sharper, you will probably notice that you are edging your outside ski a bit. That's OK.

The Step Turn

The step turn is more practical when the snow is soft, which is when the wedge turn is more difficult to use. It can, however, be used on harder snow, but it will not stop you as quickly as the wedge. It is an essential turn for all skiers, even the world class skiers use it often when they need a "sure-footed" turn.

While moving down the fall line, step out with the tip of the ski that you want to be the inside ski in your turn. The tip of the inside ski moves away from the tip of the other, but the tails stay close together. Once you have stepped with the one ski, put your weight on it and bring the other ski, the outside ski, parallel. Keep your ankles and knees flexed during the turn. Repeat the same movements until you have turned as far as you want to turn. Then practice coming back the other way. As you do this, move your shoulders, arms and hands in the direction of the turn.

The step turn is essential for all skiers

If one ski slips, take many small steps so that the skis do not separate too far and require too much of a weight shift. Keep your body partially crouched so that your hips are closer to your knees and ankles — which will be controlling your turn. As you become more advanced you can take bigger steps, but for now, keep it simple.

The step turn is accomplished in three easy steps — repeated if necessary to complete the turn.

1) Step in the direction that you want to turn. The tips of the skis must be farther apart than the tails. The ski with which you step becomes the inside of the turning arc.

2) Shift your weight quickly to the inside ski then bring the other ski up to it and parallel.

3) Repeat this action with as many quick steps as are needed to complete the turn. Beginners will take smaller steps than will more advanced skiers.

Here are three videos of the step turn and one skate turn:

Links for e-book	Url- address for printed book
Press on the link (ctrl + click)	**Write address into your web-browser**
The stepturn 1	https://vimeo.com/299301546/9d11f965e4
The stepturn 2	https://vimeo.com/299302383/8ef87fa2b7
The stepturn 3	https://vimeo.com/299304814/bca3872638
The skate turn	https://vimeo.com/299299382/993934e9db

Intermediate Turns

The Skate Turn

Start on a hill that is not too challenging until you get the feel of the turn. The skate turn is similar to the step turn, but it is more dynamic. Instead of merely stepping out on one ski, you push off the other ski as you step. The push-off ski is edged, and the body is propelled forward, diagonally toward the stepped-out ski. (See photos below.) The force of the push off brings the body over the stepped ski so the next turn step can be quickly continued. A double poling action can aid in the force and quickness of this turn.

The Skate Turn

The Swing Turn

The swing turn is a combination of the wedge and the step turn. While traversing across the mountain:

1) Lift or slide the tail of the uphill ski. This forms a wedge.

2) Put your weight on the uphill ski.

3) At the completion of the turn, the tail of the inside ski is brought inward so that you are again skiing with the skis parallel. This can be done while flattening the skis on the snow and side slipping as the parallel position is regained.

The Stem Christie

A slightly advanced method of turning, yet quite similar to the basic turn, is the "stem christie." The stem christie (sometimes called the wedge christie) combines the wedge, edging and stepping to make a higher speed turn which is effective on harder snow. The "stem" is the movement of the uphill ski outward into a modified wedge. The "christie" is named for the town where the turn was first used and popularized — Christiania. Christiania was the former name for the modern city of Oslo.

While skiing down an incline steeper than that used for the wedge turn, plant the pole near the tip of the downhill ski — the ski which will be on the inside of your turn. Step out with the ski on the other side (the uphill ski), moving the tail farther out than the tip. (This is the stem.) Put your weight on this ski and edge it so that it becomes the dominant ski. You will begin to turn in the direction that it is facing. Bring the second ski parallel with the first. Repeat the same steps so that you are stepping further across the hill. Ride the turn on the outside ski. Then bring the inside ski parallel.

If you can put your weight the inside edge of the uphill ski after you have stemmed, the turn should complete itself. (Turns which use the edging of the outside ski are more effective if the ski has a side cut. This is discussed in the chapter on equipment.)

You can do this turn by making a series of stems. In a more advanced turn you would stem, put the weight on the outside ski, and ride it around until the turn is completed.

The Parallel Turn

Parallel turns are more advanced turns which are used for wider curves and generally at higher speeds. It is often preferable when the snow is consistent but perhaps a bit slippery. The parallel turn provides a better side-to-side balance for these conditions.

A parallel turn is like a stem christie, but without the stem. Instead of stemming the skis, you will slide them. The parallel turn starts with planting the pole about even with the inside ski tip. The pole plant will be just behind the tip of the ski. The plant of the pole takes the weight off the ski next to the pole, the inside ski of the turn, and makes it easier to slide. You will be turning around the pole.

While advanced skiers will execute the turn with the skis close together, the intermediate skier will probably find it easier to keep the skis about shoulder width apart. This aids in balance, but makes it a bit harder to turn.

If you have skied Alpine, you are used to shorter poles. Because the cross country pole is longer than an Alpine pole, you will plant the pole a bit more forward. The progression is as follows:

1) Bend downward by flexing the ankles and knees.

2) Plant the pole as you extend your legs. This puts more weight on the skis but as you reach the top of the extension there is less weight on the skis so they turn more easily. As you do this your torso should move upward and forward.

3) Steer the skis in the new direction using both the knees and feet to make the turn. Emphasize turning the inside ski so that you don't bring the outside ski too wide and make the turn into a stem christie.

4) Flex the ankles and knees again to edge the skis and put more weight on them.

5) If you are going to link parallel turns going down the hill, prepare immediately for the next turn. Bend the legs, plant the pole as you extend your legs, turn the skis, then bend the legs again.

The Telemark Turn

The Telemark turn is the oldest of the high-speed turns. It was developed in the area of Telemark, 100 miles southwest of Oslo. It is used extensively on the hills in the United States and in Norway today. One of its major advantages is that it is effective in heavy deep snow or when carrying a heavy backpack. It is also used by ski jumpers to control their speed after they have landed. (We'll save ski jumping for the next book!)

The Telemark turn is a steered turn. As opposed to the other turns so far discussed, the Telemark turn does not keep the tips near each other. The inside ski is dropped far back with its tip coming close to the boot of the forward ski but angled toward the other ski.

The Telemark turn starts, as does the wedge or stem turn, with the weight on the uphill ski — the turning ski. The pole is planted as in the other high-speed turns. The inside knee of the turn drops down within a few inches of the snow in sharp turns. This is what pushes the inside ski backwards. The weight will be fairly evenly distributed between your two feet.

The amount of weight shifted and the amount of knee flex depend on the snow conditions and the degree of arc desired. In softer snow or for a longer turning radius, there would be less weight on the turning ski. Conversely, on hard snow or for quicker turns, the weight shift will be more pronounced. Of course, a ski with a greater side cut will also aid in the turn.

The wide ski position is very stable in the forward-backward dimension, but is not stable in the right-left dimension. For this reason

Telemark skiers often hold their arms outward for more balance. However, as they become more advanced, this is not necessary nor desirable.

While an Alpine skier would have the upper body facing down the hill, Telemark skiers face up the hill. For slow turns this is not so important, but for sharper turns it is critical.

To execute the Telemark turn:

1) With the torso angled just slightly forward, the outside ski (the left ski if turning right) is pushed forward.

2) As the ski is pressed forward, bend at the knee and put weight on the ski. The knee should be over the toes.

3) The inside ski slides backward and the tip points inward. (In sharp turns, the tip of the inside ski may come almost back to the boot of the outside ski.)

4) The sharper the turn, the greater the knee bend. In sharp turns, the angles at the knees may be close to 90 degrees.

5) Let your weight be primarily on your front ski. There need only be enough weight on the rear ski to control its direction. But for some turns, you will want both skis working for you. You will need to have the weight evenly distributed and the edge the turning sides of both skis — both right edges if you are turning right.

6) Steer the skis with your feet and knees to make the turn. Think of the big toe of your forward ski, and the little toe of your rear ski as steering your skis.

7) Your shoulders twist up hill; the sharper the turn, the more counter rotation of your shoulders up the hill.

In deep powder, you will weight both skis, as if you were skiing only one ski. If you are making a parallel turn, you will both weight and edge the two skis. In telemarking you will have a good deal of weight on the rear ski because it is acting as an extension of the front ski — like one long ski.

The Telemark turn is particularly useful when you need forward-backward stability. This is likely to be the case when you are skiing very deep powder, crusty snow or crud — that chopped up junky snow which we often encounter. These snow conditions may often slow your skis and throw your balance forward. The wider forward-backward base of the Telemark can reduce the problems.

Special Situations

The challenge of the steeps is that everything continually changes. Snow consistency (light or heavy), steepness, degree of friction (ice or powder), and snow composition (crud and crust) are some of the variations that you will experience. With so many variations, just one or two types of turns will not be enough for the skier who wants to challenge the mountain.

Jump turns often are the salvation for the advanced skier who is in difficult snow. These are parallel-like turns which can get you out of the difficult crud and allow you to turn in the air. Bend your knees and plant your pole, then jump from both feet. As your skis come up bend your knees even more so that you can get your skis farther from the snow. Once airborne, turn your skis in the direction you want to go, then land. Your pole plant will vary depending on the steepness of the slope. It can be as far back as your heel in steep terrain.

In very difficult snow this type of turn can be your greatest salvation. Make a series of jumps: jump turn right, then jump turn left. As you land after each turn and your knees sink down toward your skis, you will be ready for your next turn. If you are in deep crud, you may not want to link your turns, but rather traverse then make a 180-degree jump and come back the other way. It is a technique which requires practice — but when you need it you need it!

Drills

Wedge Stop

1) Slide your skis out bringing the tips close together and the tails apart. The greater the angle, the more potential stopping power.

2) Edge the inside edges of the skis by bringing the knees and ankles inward, while lowering your hips.

3) The greater the angle of the ski edges, the more potential stopping power.

4) To increase your stopping power, steer the heel of your boot more outward (for wedge width) and the ankle more inward for greater edging. Feel the pressure on the inside of your big toe so that you have more inward pressure on the inside front edges of the skis.

Sliding the Ski

1) Keeping your ski tips in approximately the same spot, slide the tail of one ski out.

2) Then follow with the other ski so that they are parallel.

3) Continue this sliding drill until the ski tails have scribed a complete circle.

4) Then go back the other way until you have another completed circle.

Edging the Ski

1) While standing on both skis, move your knees and ankles to the right slowly.

2) Then move them to the left.

3) Check the skis to see that they are edging with the movement of your ankles.

In a wedge position:

1) Lower your hips and bring both knees and ankles inward.

2) Check to see that the outside edges of the skis are moving upward.

3) Now lean forward and feel the pressure on the inside edge of the big toe.

Steering the Ski

1) Slide one ski outward about 10 inches.

2) Slide the tip out, then in. Get the feeling that your foot is steering the ski.

3) Try it with the other ski.

Stepping with the Ski

Use the same drill as the sliding drill, but lift each ski and step with it until you have completed a circle. This is called a star turn if you are not moving. When moving it is the step turn.

CHAPTER 7
Skating

For many years, skating was only used by skiers as they passed others who were skiing in the same tracks. It was also commonly used in making turns. However, it is now a technique that has become more popular for, not only racers, but recreational skiers as well. Now special wide trails are often prepared just for the skaters, while the classical skiers still ski in their two-track trails. Skating is at the same time a simple and an advanced method for cross country skiing. While on the one hand many people learn to skate much quicker than they learn the classic technique, ski racers universally will skate if it is possible. In skating the poles are longer (4 to 6 inches —10 to 15 centimeters) and shorter skis (4 to 6 inches) for skating compared with shorter poles and longer skis for classic diagonal stride skiing.

In ski races, the skaters are 10 to 30 percent faster than the classical, diagonal stride skiers. For the same amount of exertion, a skater can go at least 10 percent faster. A study of the Italian National Ski team showed that for the same speed, the skating techniques used 15 to 30 percent less energy than the classical technique. For these reasons, as you advance in skiing you will probably want to develop an efficient skating technique.

The skate is used for speed on level terrain, skiing a curve and climbing hills. Slightly different techniques are used for each — particularly in how and when the poles are planted. There are also variations in the angle of the skis, with less of an angle on the flat land but a greater angle on the steeper hills.

There are several types of skating, but different from the first types of skating technique, they are all two-sided skating and uses different poling methods. The fundamental positions and techniques are essentially the same. The techniques differ in timing and application to terrain.

The Norwegians call these techniques "dances" while the Americans and many others often label them by the "V" shape of the skis.

The different skating techniques are:

1) **Free skate, skiing without poles**
   a. When it goes too fast
   b. When you are a beginner
2) **The single dance, V1 skate**
   a. When it is flat and you are going fast
3) **The double dance, V2 skate**
   a. When it is slight uphill
4) **The paddle dance**
   a. When it is steep uphill
5) **The diagonal dance**
   a. When you skate up the monster hill in Tour The Ski
      (very steep)
6) **Maraton Skate**
   a. so old and nostalgic that it qualifies for the book

The basic V skate should start with a skier standing in a V position without poles. The skier has to edge one ski on the inside edge and at the same time push off the same ski, while transferring her/his weight on to the other ski. This motion is repeated until the skier is able to ski like this for a while without stopping. It is important to find a rhythm. This is the basics of edging and gliding. Skiing without poles also gives the skier the necessary practiceto use the legs for motion, not the poles. The skiing motion with the legs is the basic of all various V techniques used in skating.

In the past the focus has been on getting the nose, head and knee over the tip of the weighted ski, and then twisting the upper body to orientate in the direction of that ski (and away from the direction of travel). These drills can be useful for beginners, but the consequence can be too much twisting motion and overemphasis on head-oriented weight shift rather than hip or core movement. Some twisting might occur, but it should not dominate the movement.

Free skate-- using your legs only

As stated earlier, this technique is used when you go too fast to use your poles or when you are a beginner. This rarely happens at the same time, so there is no need to worry. We will first practice on the beginners, not going too fast.

As a beginner it is important to start with the basics and that is using your legs in skating. Drills such as as skiing without poles are great for building strength, weight transfer, and coordination.

Free skate is a great way to start skating, then you can try to use your arms while you ski, it will help you get motion forward.

Decisively push on one ski then you transfer yourweight to the other ski—the gliding ski. It is important to push through the heel to prevent stepping off the ski to the toes in forward direction. This will decrease the performance and speed. So push with your heels.

You can push too seldom by gliding too long. Or you can push too often with the result that you won't glide long enough. You must transfer your weight from the pushing ski to the gliding ski. This will not develop momentum forward, and is similar to spinning the tires of a car in the snow.

I have been taught to focus on the right things to do, not the don'ts. Anyhow I believe it is important to have some insight into the "wrongs" or

68

"do not's" when you try to learn something new. It is harder to relearn than to learn it properly from the start. Hope this helps a little bit.

Skating without poles

General Principles of Skating

Body Position
The body should be nearly erect, with only a slight bend at the waist. The feet should be close together to aid in power and balance.

The Eye Focus
Focus the eyes in the direction of the gliding ski — about 10 yards ahead. The eyes are crucial to balance and are essential in evaluating the upcoming terrain.

The Force Phase
It is easier to practice the force phase initially without poles. In this way, it is just about like roller or ice skating. The arms swing freely and the

legs provide the power. Just as in walking or running, the left arm swings forward forcefully as the left leg pushes back in the skating action. Then glide on the right leg for a short distance. Then push off from the right leg.

The angle of the skating ski will not be too wide as you learn to skate. It is enough that you get some edging for the backward force. As you do this, think of the hips, not the legs, as providing your power. Let the skis do the work as the big muscles of the hips force them backward.

The force phase in the skating technique will last longer than that in the classical technique. It may last well over half a second. An angle of about 30 degrees will give a sufficient force pad. Lean forward and twist your torso slightly toward the pushing ski. Leaning will edge the ski so that you can push off. As you generate more speed, the angle of the skis will be reduced. As you go up steeper hills, the angle will greatly increase.

In skating it is important to remember that you are trying to push the snow sideways. Push with the whole foot — not just the toes. In fact, it feels like you are pushing with your heel.

The Glide

The glide requires balance. The center of gravity, which is in the middle of your hips when you are standing up, moves over the gliding ski. This phase lasts from the end of the force phase of the pushing ski to the beginning of the skating force from the gliding ski. The shoulders should be perpendicular to the gliding ski to keep the body correctly aligned.

A rule which we always use is that the nose, knee and gliding ski must all be in a vertical line. This allows you to move your center of gravity effectively to the gliding ski.

The Recovery Phase

After the skating ski is pushed back in the power phase and the glide is effected, the skating leg moves forward to become the gliding ski on the next stride. In order to make certain that the legs are close it is a good idea to practice having the boot of the skating ski touch the gliding ski boot on the recovery step.

Double Poling

You have already done double poling but there are a few different concerns to consider while poling during skating. The poling action starts with your body totally erect, even on the toes. The poles are planted about 6 to 12 inches (15 to 30 cm) behind the hands. This is approximately next to the toes of the boots. Your body weight on the poles begins the thrust. You bend at the waist forcefully to develop the initial thrust.

The angle of your torso in the poling movement should be between 45 and 60 degrees. Some racers will bend to 90 degrees at the start to develop maximum power. The elbow will now be flexed about 90 degrees. The final thrust is then performed by the muscles of the upper back and shoulders (latissimus dorsi and posterior deltoids) and the back of the upper arm (triceps). The triceps extend the arm fully in the final thrust. Your hands are close to your knees, maybe below your knees. The arms then move forward in the recovery phase with the pole tips staying close to the snow.

Different Variations of Skating

Let's introduce the different techniques with poles, but remember that even skiers with ambitions and good technique practice skiing without poles.

The single dance, V1 skate

The V1 is a high-speed technique used on the flat and when there is a slope of few degrees. The snow should be fast (old snow). For many skaters the single dance technique is the fastest for the slight downhill path. The V1 skate uses a double pole plant for every other skating move. So the pole plant would come on every right skate or on every left skate. (In the V1 there is only one double pole plant for a complete skating cycle of two skates — a right and a left.)

> *The timing for V1 is:*
> *Double pole and skate with right ski — glide on the left ski — skate with left ski — glide on the right ski*

V1, single dance, right side double pole

From the pictures above you can see that the skier will pole on every right skate, the poles will be planted with the arms outstretched and the poles angled backward so that the plant is near the toe binding. The plant must be close to the skis.

The body bends forward applying the body weight to the poles as the right ski begins to skate. The angle of the skate will be less than 30 degrees. The angle will be greater if going uphill and will be less if the skier is moving fast, such as downhill. The reduced angle allows for a longer skating stride.

The gliding ski (left ski) will be angled slightly outward, not straight ahead as in the marathon skate. As the right leg finishes its kick, the skier glides until the momentum slows then kicks back with the left ski, which will have a slightly larger angle. The poles are recovered and made ready for the next pole plant. Good skaters can go 8 to 10 yards per single stride, even on a slight uphill, using this technique.

Here are three videos of V1, single dance:

72

Links for e-book	Url- address for printed book
Press on the link (ctrl + click)	**Write address into your web-browser**
V1 single dance right side	https://vimeo.com/299497728/ec1600af70
V1 single dance left side	https://vimeo.com/299495897/a650827e31
V1 single dance right side	https://vimeo.com/299499660/db81fe17c7

The double dance, V2 skate

The double dance (V2 technique) uses a double pole plant on each skating move — left and right pushes. The pole plant precedes the push off of the skating ski.

This is probably the fastest skating technique if you are going slightly uphill, but it is difficult because it requires great balance and it can be more exhausting. One double poling occurs with the beginning of each skate when the legs are together. It is used primarily in uphill skiing which is a little steeper than that for which the V1 is used. Fast old snow is also a big plus if you are going to use this technique.

The timing for V2 is:
* Double pole and skate with right ski — glide on the left ski — then double pole and skate with left ski — glide on the right ski

73

V2, double dance skate

The poles are planted, as in all double poling, quite close to the toe binding of the boots. The body, which weights the poles, is similar to that of the single dance (V1). In high-speed skiing, the angle of the torso to the thighs may vary from 15 to nearly 90 degrees through the cycle.

The angle of the skating ski will vary with the speed and the frequency of skates — the number of skates per minute. The faster the frequency of the skating strides, the greater the angle of the skating ski. The longer the strides, the less the angle — somewhere around 15 degrees.

For most of the stride only one ski is on the snow. Then there is that period when both poles are in the air recovering, and you are riding only on the gliding ski — so good balance is essential.

The center of gravity (the center of the hips) must flow smoothly from one ski to the other without too much movement to the side or without excessive up and down movement. This is a major factor in making this technique the most difficult to learn effectively.

Here are five videos of V2, double dance:

74

Links for e-book	Url- address for printed book
Press on the link (ctrl + click)	**Write address into your web-browser**
V2 double dance, easy terrain 1	https://vimeo.com/299510041/ba8b141dcb
V2 double dance, easy terrain 2	https://vimeo.com/299501627/34487535c6
V2 double dance semi flat 1	https://vimeo.com/299503643/e6c625fddc
V2 double dance semi flat 2	https://vimeo.com/299505460/82c3a62d94
V2 double dance, semi flat 3	https://vimeo.com/299508685/bad5a381b4

The paddle dance

The paddle dance is superior on steep uphill climbs when racing in competition. It is a difficult technique to master, but when learned it offers the skier more effective balance throughout the cycle — as opposed to the double dance which requires the better balance. The paddle dance can also be used on the flat when the snow is slower.

As said before, the technique gets its name from the fact that the arm action resembles that of a canoeist, with one arm starting downward before the other does. The poling is always timed with the ski on one side — as in the single dance (V1) technique. The ski which is timed with the first pole plant is called the "drive" ski. The other is called the "hang" ski. If there is a slope coming from one side, in addition to the slope you are climbing, the "hang" side ski will generally be on that uphill slope side.

The paddle technique is as follows:

1) The drive ski begins its push with a slight angle (generally 12 to 15 degrees). The grip of the pole on that side is brought close to the midline of the body and planted quite far back with nearly a 30-degree angle backward to reach the toe of the near boot which has already begun its backward movement. The other ski, the "hang" ski, is being brought forward and is either just about to be set in the snow or has just hit the snow.

2) The second pole (the hang side pole) is quickly planted next to the heel of the near boot (the hang side boot). Its angle backward is only about 15 degrees because it is reaching for the ski which has just been planted uphill. The pole is pushed backward as the hang side ski takes a short glide and the body weight is shifted to the gliding ski. Both poles should be pushing in the direction of the glide of the hang ski.

3) The hang-side ski begins its skate with a sharper outward angle (20 to 30 degrees), and the poles are recovering, ready for the next plants. (The recovery should be low without an upward movement of the pole baskets.) The glide on the drive ski will be 10 to 20 percent longer than that on the hang ski. The weight is shifted to the gliding ski in preparation for the next skate.

The Padle Dance, right side pole plant

The steeper the uphill slope the greater the outward angle of the skis and the less glide will be experienced. Meanwhile, the forward steps taken in the uphill movement are very long — the longest of any skating technique. When used on steep uphills, the steps are quick, and there is little glide. When used on flatter areas or on faster snow, the glides will be much longer.

> **The timing for the paddle dance is:**
> *Poles (left, right)— skate left — glide on right ski — skate right ski — glide on left ski

Here are a few videos of the paddle dance:

Links for e-book	Url- address for printed book
Press on the link (ctrl + click)	Write address into your web-browser
Paddle dance left side 1	https://vimeo.com/299306425/5b88397220
Paddle dance left side 2	https://vimeo.com/299309738/4b06ee8288
Paddle dance left side 3	https://vimeo.com/299311995/94643380cc
Paddle dance right side	https://vimeo.com/299315914/0a95cf118f
Paddle dance right side	https://vimeo.com/299320756/5721b7c4d5
Paddle dance right side	https://vimeo.com/299322182/7fbbf292ef
Paddle jump	https://vimeo.com/299324014/3eeacd03fd

The Diagonal Dance (Diagonal V)

The diagonal dance is used often for steep uphill climbs. It is similar to the herringbone, but there is a gliding phase with each step, and the pole action is single — that is, it is like the classic diagonal skiing technique where the left arm poles while the right ski skates, then the right arm poles while the left ski skates. This technique is used for even steeper hill climbing than are the previously mentioned techniques. It is not used often in World Cup meets, because the skiers are so strong that they do well with the other techniques. But there is one exception, and that is when they skate up the "monster hill" in Tour The Ski.

This is the final race of the tour and goes up the downhill in Cavalese, Italy. It is located on the mountain Alpe Cermis, 2250 meters above sea level, and is the steepest slope that has ever been included in the World Cup in cross-country skiing. The entire run is nine kilometers long, while the actual hill is 3.6 kilometers. The skiers climb 420 meters in height, with a slope up to 28 percent. When a hill as steep as this even professional skiers use the diagonal V (dance).

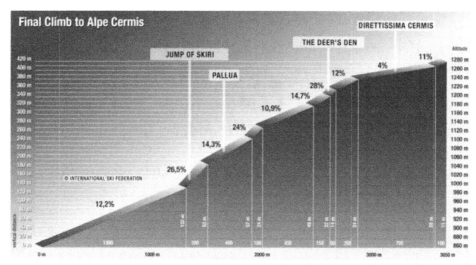

When used for hill climbing, the skis' angle are much greater than the shallow angles used for skating on the flats and on moderate downhills. The angle of the ski from the direction of motion can be more than 30 degrees and as much as 45 degrees.

Because the skating is forceful, the upper body will rotate somewhat with the shoulder on the poling side reaching toward the skating ski side. From this forward position, the pole is planted near the heel of the boot to give a better angle of drive from the arm push. The rotation of the upper body is greater than in other skating styles because of the single poling technique.

Because of the uphill climb, the torso may be inclined farther forward. While some skaters keep their bodies nearly erect, others will bend to near 60 degrees. On the other hand, when used on the flats or slight downhills, the skater may nearly tuck and may, or may not, pole.

The diagonal V is one of the better ways for beginners to learn to skate. Without poles it develops the basic skating pattern, and with poles the timing is similar to the classic technique — which the beginner has already learned. It is less strenuous than the paddle dance for uphill skiing. And without poling, it allows for normal body coordination which is used in walking and running. The major disadvantage would be for those who want to attain a higher speed because the side-to-side movement of the diagonal dance reduces the forward speed.

78

> **The timing for diagonal dance is:**
>
> ** Right skate, left pole — short glide on left — left skate, right pole — short glide on right.*

Marathon Skate, one-side skating

Marathon skate is a very old technique, but was revolutionary when introduced. It was the start of cross country skating, and faster than diagonal striding. The man who started it all was Bill Koch from USA who introduced skating in the World Cup with great success.

To use this technique, start with both skis parallel and both poles planted. It will be often used if you are skating in tracks. The weight is partially shifted to the ski which will push. The torso bends downward as the poling action begins and the skating ski is forced backward. At the end of the force phase the skating ski and the poles recover and the skier glides on the gliding ski. When the momentum begins to slow, the same process is repeated with the same skating ski.

The sequence is as follows:

1) Poles are planted and the tip of the skating ski is lifted outward to about 30 degrees.

2) The torso bends forward at the waist and begins the push backward on the poles and the skating ski pushes backward.

3) The torso continues to bend (while the arms push the poles to the end of the thrust) and the skating ski finishes its force phase.

4) The skating ski and the arms recover to the original position and the glide continues on the gliding ski.

When skating a curve or skiing uphill, the cycle (from pole plant to pole plant) is increased — with more rapid kicking and poling. When skiing slightly downhill the cycle can be slowed.

The one-sided skate is reasonably fast and can be used in a narrower area than can the double-sided skating techniques. It is also quite fast when skiing a curve — with the inside ski used as the gliding ski. And in slight downhill runs it is fast, particularly if done in a tuck and without poling. However, it is not as effective as other skating techniques in going up a steeper incline, and if there is no track, the gliding ski is more difficult to control. In racing it is used only when the snow in the track is faster than the snow on the path.

Many ski areas have flat areas tailored to the skating skier. In other places you will probably ski in the tracks. To skate in the tracks, using the marathon skate, lift one leg out of the tracks and angle it so that the tip is farther away from the tracks than the tail is. You won't need to worry about getting the force ski out of the way of the gliding ski, because the gliding ski will be deeper since it is in the track. Take several skates with one ski while gliding on the other, then put the skating ski in the track and skate with the other ski.

Your longer poles should easily reach behind the angled ski. Plant both poles behind the ski and push off on the force ski. Your hips will be closer to the angled ski because you will be pushing hard for power. As soon as the power is developed bring the hips back over the gliding ski.

As mentioned in the chapter about classical skiing double poling has replaced diagonal stride in many marathon races, even WC classical races. The Marathon skate is probably used as often as the skiers can, without being penalized for skating (which is not allowed when skiing in a classical race).

Common Errors in Skating

• The center of gravity moves up and down. There should be little up and down movement, only forward and side-to-side movement. Each additional and unnecessary movement impedes balance.

• Keeping a stance too wide during the skate without bringing the feet together. An excessively wide base requires that the center of gravity be shifted too far on each stride. This makes it much more difficult to balance.

• "Sitting," which brings the center of gravity (the hips) over the heels, reduces the chance for an effective force phase in the skate. It is not only inefficient but it takes a great deal of energy to hold a sitting position.

• Planting the poles inside the angled ski can trip the skier.

• Kicking only with the toes or the balls of the feet instead of with the whole foot is also inefficient.

A Final Note on Skating

As mentioned earlier, even beginners can start with skating — and may find it easier than the classic diagonal stride technique. When you see good skiers skating, the ease and freedom of the movement, and the joy of that freedom, becomes apparent. In Norway, all of the good young skiers skate whether or not they are in competition. As you watch them fly around the tracks at Holmenkollen or pass you on the trails of Nordmarka, you get the feeling that they are flying on skis. And when you begin to do it yourself, you'll enjoy that same exhilarating feeling!

CHAPTER 8
The Mechanics of Skiing

There are a number of mechanical factors that you may want to understand relating to skiing. You need to consider: friction between your skis and the snow, forces generated by your arms and legs, what happens when you turn, and many other variables relative to the science of skiing. You may want to increase your understanding of these in order to ski more effectively. If you are not so interested in the "whys" and "wherefores" of skiing and are only interested in the "how to's," you can skip this chapter.

As you get more proficient at skiing techniques, you will want to become more efficient. Elements, such as reducing drag by being in a more aerodynamic position or by having a better glide with your skis, are important. On the other hand, having the necessary friction under the power ski and having the leg and arm strength to maximize the push are also important. Let us look at a few of the components of the laws of physics and kinesiology that you will want to consider as you begin to increase your skiing ability.

Factors Affecting Balance

Gravity

Gravity is the pull of the earth on the skier. In simple terms, it is what you weigh. If you were skiing in outer space, you would be nearly weightless. But since most of your skiing will be on the planet Earth, you will be pulled toward the center of our world.

If it weren't for gravity, there would be no reason to learn technique. Without gravity one stride would develop a glide that would never stop. Such efficiency might be enjoyable for a while, but it would do nothing for your physical fitness and would soon be quite boring! Of course, gravity lessens when you go downhill and increases when you go uphill.

Gravity is also slightly affected by latitude — the closer you are to the equator the less there is. It is 0.005 less at the equator than the North Pole. So a skier in Oslo, Norway, would have to work about 0.4 percent harder to achieve the same speed as a skier in Quito, Ecuador. Additionally, there are factors of wind and snow friction (drag) which can aid a skier in Norway going downhill. The skier in Oslo would go about 0.2 percent faster downhill than the skier in Quito. On the other hand, the lesser gravity in Quito would make the equipment weigh 0.4 percent less, so climbing a hill would be easier near the equator. You can probably balance these two factors if you do your cross country skiing in Florida or the Caribbean!

81

Yet while the effect of gravity is actually the major factor related to ski speed, there are other ingredients.

Center of gravity

Balance and Your Center of Gravity

The longer the ski stride and glide, the better your balance must be. Balance is achieved when the center of gravity of the body is exactly over the supporting foot or feet.

The center of gravity is where the exact center of the body's weight is concentrated. The pull of the earth's gravitational forces is centered in this part of your body. If you were to stick an imaginary needle through the middle of the body and the body were perfectly balanced, your body would spin effortlessly around that point. You would have pierced the center of gravity.

If you were to balance a baseball bat on your finger, you will find that your finger will be farther away from the grip of the bat because there is less wood (weight) there. In fact, your finger may be two-thirds of the way toward the wide end of the bat. When you have balanced the bat, the center of gravity of the bat will be directly over your finger.

If you are standing erect, your center of gravity will generally be in the area of your hips. Most women have a center of gravity a bit lower than do men. A person with thin legs, but a heavy upper body would have a center of gravity higher than a person with a light upper body and heavy legs. If you bend forward with a 90-degree angle at your hips, your center of gravity will be outside your body and in front of the hips.

Balance and Your Base of Support

Your base is the foot, or feet, on which your weight is supported. In skiing down the fall line, it is equally balanced on both feet. If you are in a glide, it is totally on the gliding foot. If your center of gravity is not directly over the exact middle of your base, you will fall. If it goes too far past your base, you fall outward. If it doesn't go far enough, you fall inward. If it is too far back, you fall backward. And if it is too far forward, you fall forward. But because your feet are longer than they are wide, you have much less of a chance of falling forward or backward than you do to your side.

If you stand on one foot and do not fall, it means that your center of gravity is exactly over the base of support of your foot. However if you are walking, you don't shift your center of gravity totally over the supporting foot. It never quite gets there. Before you fall your other foot hits the ground, and you regain your balance. You are also aided by the muscles contracting on the outside of the supporting leg. They prevent your body from collapsing inward and falling away from the supporting leg.

The key to balance is being able to smoothly get your center of gravity exactly over the middle of your support base. The longer the glide, the more important this is. If you are taking short choppy steps up a hill in a herringbone series of strides, your center of gravity does not have to be transferred to the exact center of the base. This is because before you fall you have regained your balance by putting your weight on the other leg —just like in walking. But if the hill is steep, you will want all of your center of gravity on the pushing ski so that you can get the maximum amount of push on the snow.

If you were making quick turns while coming down a hill, you would lean into one turn, then quickly lean the other way as you make a turn in the other direction. Your center of gravity would not move out to the outside ski. Before you fell inward, you would make another turn which would catch your balance. If you have watched Alpine skiers, you would notice that the slalom skier, who makes very quick turns, always has his or her center of gravity inside of the feet.

But the downhill skier, who makes few turns, will be pretty well balanced on both legs most of the time. During a series of quick turns, the centrifugal force of the turn pulls your body outward. If it gets as far as your outside ski, you would fall outward. So, when turning, your center of gravity will not get quite out over the outside ski. It's just like riding a bicycle around a corner, you lean into the turn or you fall outward. But if you leaned when going straight, you would fall inward. So, where you hold your center of gravity in order to keep your balance depends on whether you are going straight or turning and how high your center of gravity is over your skis.

In skiing you need to be able to develop the coordination that allows you to shift your center of gravity as far toward the supporting leg as is necessary for the length of your stride. The longer stride and glide require a more complete shift of the center of gravity over the supporting foot. And certainly, you must be able to control the lateral movement of the center of gravity so that it never gets outside of your base or — down you go!

Friction

When gliding you want as little friction as possible. When generating force in the push-off ski, you want a great deal of friction. (For you engineers and physicists — a well-waxed ski has a coefficient of friction of about 0.05; the power ski in classical skiing must have a coefficient of at least 0.2 in the middle section of the ski when power is applied, and in skating, where the ski edge is dug into the snow, the value can come close to 1.0.)

What this means in practice is that, if you are skiing the classical diagonal technique, you must know how much of your ski is coming in contact with the snow when you push off. That part of the base of your ski must have a wax or a texture (waxless skis) which will give maximum friction. Then, when you glide you want that high friction wax to be off of the snow so that it does not create a hydrodynamic drag. And if you are skating, you can use a glide wax over your whole ski so that friction can be reduced when you glide.

Newer snow creates more drag than does older snow. The older snow has often undergone thawing and refreezing, or if it is in a track, has been compressed many times. The millions of individual flakes in new fallen snow, with each flake having six points, create more drag by having more "sharp" points in contact with the gliding ski. The individual flakes of the snow are compressed into larger crystals with fewer points to produce friction on the ski bottoms. And, of course, ice has even fewer contact points so glide is greatly enhanced by ice.

But the same characteristics of ice make it much more difficult to overcome the lack of friction (between the ice and the ski) with the pushing ski. The wax of the classical skier and the edge of the skater get far less grip on ice.

Drag

Drag is what slows you down. There are two kinds of drag. Hydrodynamic drag is the friction developed as the ski glides over the snow, along with the friction created by the thin layer of water which forms as the ski melts the snow under it.

Hydrodynamic drag is the result of increased friction between the ski and the thin coating of water under the ski. That water can become much thicker when skiing in warmer temperatures, such as occurs in the spring. And the thicker water can create a "suction" effect which greatly slows down the ski. Ski manufacturers have worked to develop structures for the bases for the skis which break up this suction effect.

Aerodynamic drag is the resistance of the air and wind against your body. When your speed doubles, your drag factor increases by 400 percent. A wind from the front increases aerodynamic drag while a wind from back reduces it. The more surface area your body uses to push against the air, the more drag you produce. Obviously that is why a tuck position when going downhill reduces drag. In fact, the tuck reduces wind resistance by more than 50 percent. (And that approximate 55 percent reduction in aerodynamic drag is multiplied by the square of the speed, so the faster you go the more important it is to be in an aerodynamic position.)

Aerodynamics taken seriously

This tri-athlete is taking aerodynamics to a new level. For more inspiration look at: https://triallan.com/

Clothing can reduce drag. Runners and cyclists have found that certain clothing can reduce drag by up to 10 percent. Tighter fitting clothing and a drag reducing hood can be obvious drag reducing aids. You have certainly seen the Olympic ice skaters wearing very tight body suits and head hoods. Ski racers have adopted the full body suits, but do not use the drag reducing hoods.

The Total Energy Consumption

The energy consumption negative factors have been calculated by Dr. Erik Spring, professor of applied physics at the University of Helsinki in

Finland. He is the scientific advisor to the Finnish world class skiers. His research indicates that the energy output of a skier is approximately:

- 30 percent to overcome the friction of the snow.
- 15 percent to overcome drag.
- 10 percent to move the skis forward after each power step.
- 5 percent to move the poles forward.

Decreasing the amount of friction by 10 percent reduces the output of energy by three percent. Similarly, a decrease in the energy consumption in any of these areas results in greater speed and efficiency. Better wax and more efficient waxing techniques are the major concerns here. But lighter skis and poles will also have an effect. So will more drag resistant clothes and a body position which will reduce drag.

In the 1980 Olympics, one of Finland's best skiers lost a race by 1/100th of a second. His long hair and beard had created more than enough drag to make that difference. In fact they were probably responsible for several yards difference in his race.

Overcoming Friction and Drag Resistance

Force

Force is the power generated which overcomes the friction of the snow and the drag of the air. Force is generated by the transfer of muscle power to the poles and the skis.

It is not only the amount of force and the angle of force which is important, but also the length of time that the force is applied to the snow. So, while a pole plant at a great angle backward would be more efficient in transferring muscle power to overcome the snow's friction, a longer poling action will apply that force longer. The new powerful style of double poling is challenging the traditional longer poling style.

Through the Poles

Obviously, the amount of force you can exert backward is the amount of force you will generate forward. We all remember Newton's third law of motion, where every action has an equal and opposite reaction. If you pushed on a pole which was perfectly vertical, you would have a resultant force which would be straight up. If you are using your poles to assist with a turn, your skis will more easily slide around the turn (side slip). Use such a pole plant in a parallel turn or a stem christie.

Of course, most of the force which you want exerted through the poles is horizontal force — force directly horizontal and parallel with the snow. In order to have such a force, you would have to have a strong vertical wall to push against with your poles parallel to the snow. Naturally, this can never happen on the snow. None of our poling during skiing will ever be exactly vertical or horizontal. The closer your hands are to the snow, the more horizontal force is exerted because the poles are more horizontal. Consequently, as the poling stroke nears its finish, when your torso is bent lower and your hands are lower, the greater the potential of force that can be transferred through the poles. A skier will therefore never put the poles in the snow in a vertical plant. So when the objective is to move forward efficiently, the pole tips should always be behind your wrists.

Full torso flexion and complete extension of the arms results in a longer poling action finishing with the poles nearly parallel to the snow for maximum force.

Because there are two factors which affect the force transmitted through the poles (the angle of the pole plant and a longer poling action), the efficient skier must find the happy medium. If the objective is to move forward, the pole must always be planted at some angle backward.

The longer poles of the skater were designed to allow for a pole plant behind the ski which is farther away from the body. But the effect has been to give the skater a more efficient transmission of power through a pole which is set at a sharper angle to the snow than the shorter poles of the classical skier. So the skater can have just as long a poling action as the classical skier yet have the poles at a more effective angle to transmit that force throughout the arm stroke. But in addition to the more effective pole angle, the skater can actually take a longer poling stroke and apply force over a longer period of time.

If the pole plant moves the snow backward and therefore slips in the snow, the amount of potential force is reduced because friction (the "sticking" factor) is reduced. If one is poling on ice and the pole does not penetrate, there is likewise less friction so less force is exerted against the snow.

Another crucial factor in the application of force through the poles is the strength of the muscles of the upper back and the back of the upper arm, the latissimus dorsi and the triceps. Developing strength (the amount of force which can be developed in one contraction of a muscle) and muscular endurance (the number of repetitions the muscle group can accomplish without tiring) are both essential. Exercises for these muscle groups are discussed in Chapter 11.

The Swedish professor Bengt Saltin, in his keynote address at the International Congress on Skiing and Science in Arlberg, Austria, in 1996, said that the amount of energy expended on the arms or legs is about equal to the power and speed output. So don't underestimate the force potential of your poling action.

A Classical Skier's Show of Force

The classical skier's force is directly backward, and the glide directly forward. Such movements should be ideal. The problem is that the force ski or kicking ski will tend to slip backward a bit; this reduces the push, and the gliding ski may be slowed if the grip wax touches the snow and increases friction.

A Skating Skier's Show of Force

The skating skier gets a better grip on the snow by angling the ski outward. The farther out it is angled, the less distance through which force can be applied and the greater the angle in the opposite direction that the gliding ski must take. Because of the greater separation of the skis during the skating movements, the center of gravity must move farther laterally than it does in classical skiing. This may create a balance problem, particularly if the glide is long.

Lift

When you are coming downhill in a tuck position, with the back rounded, you can get a slight lift from the air moving quickly over the back. This is the same principle which is used in airplane wings and which lifts the plane (the Bernoulli Principle). Bicycle racers work very hard at getting an aerodynamic position with lift. An effective position can increase efficiency 10 to 20 percent. For the skier, the lift will reduce the friction of the snow.

Energy Expenditure

Body Mass

The weight of your body and your ski equipment is important for a couple of reasons. The more your leg, boot and ski weigh, the more energy you must exert to move that leg forward. When striding forward, your leg goes about twice as fast as your torso. Then, as you push off with the leg, your foot is nearly stationary. So you must drive the leg forward then have it stop. This is a major factor in energy expenditure and in fatigue. Using the skating technique is less costly in terms of these energy expenditure factors, which is another reason for skating being faster.

When you must lift a leg, such as when climbing hills, there is a greatly increased effect of fatigue. In addition to these forward (horizontal) movements, there is an energy cost in any rotational movement which the body performs.

While this would appear to favor the smaller skier, this is not the case. Larger skiers, because of greater muscle power, seem to be able to generate more power in nearly all areas of skiing, except when skiing uphill. The primary concern is whether the skier can generate more power than the resistances (air and snow) give friction.

Since it requires more force to move a greater body weight forward, your body weight does have a negative component. Also, the more you bend at the waist, the more energy that is expended to energize your back muscles which must hold up your torso. But the bent position reduces air drag. So if you are not going too fast, your body can be more erect to save the energy expenditure in your back muscles and to reduce fatigue.

The more erect position can also be used when going uphill, because the wind resistance is not very great. In addition, by being erect the center of gravity remains more effectively over the driving ski than it would be if the skier were bent forward. This should increase the ski's ability to develop maximum friction and a more effective push off.

A heavier skier also uses more energy when in a tuck position, because the muscles of the back and thighs need to support more weight. But the effect of gravity in generating more downhill speed may more than compensate for that energy expenditure. Also, because the heavier skier will undoubtedly have a greater cross sectional area creating wind resistance and drag, the tuck position should be more valuable in reducing those drag effects.

Increasing the Efficiency of Movement

To reduce the energy expended, the efficient skier will reduce the amount of weight lifted — body weight, ski and boot weight, and pole weight.

It is impossible to eliminate all up and down movement, but keep it to a minimum. Take a look at the videos below:

Here are two videos of the diagonal stride:

Links for e-book	Url- address for printed book
Press on the link (ctrl + click)	Write address into your web-browser
Diagonal stride uphill 1	https://vimeo.com/298341392/b11f48009c
Diagonal stride slight uphill 1	https://vimeo.com/298241932/b160222ebe

If the body's center of gravity is raised and lowered often, each time it is raised muscular energy must be expended by the leg and hip muscles. So the skier must determine whether the up-down movement, such as is used in double poling, increases the speed sufficiently to make up for the increased energy expenditure.

Side-to-side movement of the center of gravity, which is much greater in skaters than in classical skiers, also increases energy expenditures. As the center of gravity is moved to the gliding ski, muscular energy is used to both move it and to stop it. However, the other positive forces in skating somewhat compensate for this problem.

To keep your movements efficient, the skis should be kept close to the snow so that energy is not wasted in lifting them excessively. Beginning classical skiers often lift the skis, rather than slide them when moving them forward. Skaters, in recovering their skis from the push off to the glide phase, may lift the ski higher than it needs to be to clear the snow.

The pole baskets should also be kept close to the snow in recovery. For every inch or centimeter they are lifted, additional energy is used.

Weight shift to get the head and center of gravity over the gliding ski

Increasing the Efficiency of the Body

The more force the legs and arms can generate in pushing the body forward, the faster you can go. Muscular strength in certain muscle groups is required for this. Continuing this pushing action over thousands of repetitions requires both muscular endurance (endurance within the appropriate muscles) and cardiopulmonary endurance (endurance related to the heart and the oxygen-carrying capacity of the blood). Both of these will be discussed more fully in Chapter 11 as well.

Getting Even More Technical!

If you want to measure yourself against the best in the world, an analysis of World Cup racers was presented by Professor Ansgar Schwirtz of the Institute of Sports and Science at the International Congress on Skiing and Science in 1996. The accompanying chart summarizes his findings:

- The speed (cycle velocity) was 7.1 meters per second for men and 6.0 for women.

- The cycle time (full two skate sequence) 1.117 seconds for men and 1.09 for women.

You can figure out the rest from the figures. Basically, the men are stronger and travel faster, but the women increase their speed of strides (cycle time) to attempt to compensate.

So if you are a man and travel at seven meters per second or a woman travelling at six meters per second, join the World Cup racers.

Comparison of men and women in stride, frequency, etc.					
Parameter	unit	male (n=14)		female (n=19)	
		X	s	X	s
cycle velocity	[m/s]	7.1	0.3	6.0**	0.3
cycle time	[s]	1.17	0.08	1.09**	0.05
cycle rate	[1/min]	51.3	3.4	55.4**	2.4
Ski-phases					
-thrust time	[s]	0.48	0.07	0.43*	0.05
-gliding time	[s]	0.69	0.06	0.65*	0.05
-thurst/cycle time	Fol	40.7	4.6	39.1	5.3
-gliding/cycle time pole- ses	[Vol	59.3	4.6	60.8	4.3
-pole left	[s]	0.27	0.03	0.31**	0.03
-pole left/cycle time	[%]	23.3	2.6	28.7**	1.9
-pole left/thrust ski	[%]	56.3	7.0	72.1**	9.2
-pole right	[s]	0.28	0.04	0.32**	0.03
-pole right/cycle time	[%]	23.4	3.5	29.4**	2.2
-pole right/thrust ski	[%]	58.3	9.6	74.4**	10.4

* significant difference to the mean value male, $p<.05$

x* significant difference to the mean value male, $p<.01$

CHAPTER 9
Equipment

The earliest known ski was used 4,500 years ago. It was a bit over four feet long and five inches wide. Other skis were more than six feet long (two meters) and weighed six pounds (2.7 kg) per pair. Until about 100 years ago, skis were made of a single piece of birch, pine, hickory or other available wood. As skiing became more popular, the wooden wheel makers also made skis.

In the late 1800s, ski manufacturing factories were developed, and soon laminated wood skis appeared. These were lighter than the solid wood skis. By the 1970s, synthetic materials found their place. Each development has allowed the skier to ski better on stronger, better shaped and technically superior equipment. And you are the beneficiary of this progress.

In 1974 the first fiberglass ski with a polyethylene base became the first of the synthetic skis. Now, with combinations of carbon fibers, Kevlar, fiberglass, acrylic foam and other modern materials, strong, lightweight skis are the order of the day. Today's skis weigh less than a third of what the older solid wood skis weighed.

With the additional reduction of the weight of boots and bindings, skiers today achieve nearly a 15 percent energy savings when skiing the same speed as a skier of 50 years ago.

Technical facts about skis

The shovel is the turned up front end of the ski. The shovel height indicates how high the shovel tip is from the main part of the ski. The tail is the rear end of the ski.

The side cut, or side camber, is the inward curve of the side of the ski from the shovel to the tip. The deeper this cut the greater the ability to turn. The bottom camber is the arch upward from the bottom of the tip to the bottom of the tail.

Length

Some prehistoric skis had a long and a short ski so that the skier could push off on the short ski then glide on the long ski. Today, we use shorter skis for skating, because they are easier to push off with and longer skis for better glide in classical skiing. The skating skis will be about 4 to 6 inches (10 to 15 cm) shorter than the classic skis.

A longer ski is more stable when moving forward, gives a greater floating effect — with less weight per square inch on the snow — and would be faster in straight ahead gliding. However, it is less maneuverable and more difficult to turn than shorter skis.

Width

The body of the skis, which had been as wide as 5 inches (12 cm) to allow it to float on the powder, has been reduced to $1^3/_4$ to $2^1/_2$ inches (4.5 to 6 cm) as machine-packed trails have become common. A wider ski is more stable but is more difficult to control when traversing a slope. Measured at the waist (the middle of the ski); racing skis are about $1^3/_4$ inches (44-45 mm) wide; touring skis vary from $1^3/_4$ to $2^1/_4$ inches (45 to 55 mm); and downhill skis such as Telemark are about $2^1/_4$ inches (55 mm) to slightly wider.

Edges

The edges can be the same material as the base or can be metal. The metal edges are primarily for mountain skiing and provide a better grip for more control, but add weight to the ski which will make it a bit slower. Where turning is important the metal is preferable, but if you are just skiing in prepared tracks you are generally better to opt for the lighter skis.

Shape

The shape of the ski allows for better turning. While competition skis have nearly parallel sides with the width of the ski decreasing slightly towards the front and back, recreational skis may have a reduced width in the middle allowing for better turning (a ski with a wider front and back).

Bottom Camber

The bottom camber (or arch) is evident when the ski is lying flat on the ground. Only a small part of the tip and tail should be touching the ground.

Stiffness

The stiffness of the ski is important because, if it bends too easily when you put weight on it, the sticky kicking area of the ski (the wax pocket) will touch the snow and will limit your glide. If it does not bend enough when you have nearly all of your weight on it, your kicking area will not make contact with the snow so you will not be able to generate power.

Side Cut

The side cut (waisting) allows for easier turning. The deeper the arc from the tip to the tail, with the middle being the narrowest, the quicker the ski can turn. The side cut for Alpine slalom skis is very great, because they are required to turn quickly. With Alpine racing skis, such as those used in Olympic racing, there is little or no side cut. This is also true for the Nordic cross country skis.

The side cut helps in turning, because when the full weight of the person is put on the inside edge of one ski, the arc of the side cut makes the ski follow that arc and turn. So if you put your weight on the inside edge of the right ski, the ski would turn toward the left. The greater the degree of arc, the tighter the ski will turn. A ski without sidecut performs well in set track. A ski with sidecut turns well

Considerations when buying skis

First determine the type of ski that you want. Mountain or Telemark skis are wider and have metal edges. They are therefore more stable and easier to turn, but they are heavier. The narrow trail skis are lighter but not quite as stable or responsive. If you are going to do all of your skiing on the mountain then the mountain skis are more appropriate.

Racing skis are quite narrow and require good balance. They are very light and very fast — if you can ski them. Touring skis are about halfway between the mountain and the racing skis. Neither of these has metal edges. There are also other types of skis.

If you skate, you may consider skis made especially for skating with reinforced sides to reduce the wear from the continued pushoffs of the skater. Beginners may want to stay with a wider ski for balance, but advanced skaters will opt for the racing type skis. Skaters will also usually use shorter skis.

And there is more, you have the choice between waxable and waxless skis. The modern waxless skis have "skin" mounted in the kick-wax area, and all you have to do is to clean the skin and apply silicone a few times each season. The older waxless ski has a moulded-in grip pattern in this area, and it looks a bit like fish-shells. This kind of waxless ski is replaced by those with skin. Skin skis offer the convenience of not having to apply kick wax every time you want to go out skiing.

When buying new skis I recommend getting a professional hotwax application on the base of the skis. This will provide you with better glide and also contribute to preventing your new skis from getting dry and white. You can also use a liquid glide wax that` you can apply yourself. It will only last an afternoon, and has to be applied every time you go out. Glide wax is useful for both waxable and waxless skis.

Waxable skis are for those who want performance, even though the performance of waxless-skin-skis are almost as good as waxable skis today.. Because the snow can vary in many ways (wetness, temperature, icy conditions), the proper wax will give you better performance.

Next determine the length of ski you want. Longer skis will give you more float and glide and will be faster, but they are more difficult to maneuver. If you plan to skate, you will want shorter skis. For classical skiing, the most common method of determining length is to stand with your arm stretched upward. With the tail of the ski on the ground, the tip should come somewhere between your wrist and your palm. Lighter people can use shorter skis if they wish. Skating skis are usually about 4 to 6 inches (10 to 15 cm) shorter than the touring ski.

Stiffness

It is important that the skis you used are matched to your size and weight. This is especially important when considering stiffness and camber (the upward arch in the middle of the skis). When you place all your weight on one ski, the camber should flatten out. If the camber doesn't flatten out, you are probably too light for the skis. On the other hand, if your partial weight on the ski flattens out the camber completely, you are too heavy for the skis. Most sporting goods stores have ways of measuring this and will help you find the right ski for you.

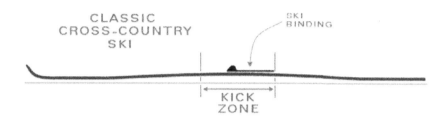

Find the ski with the proper stiffness (or flex). Have the ski shop expert pick a ski that is probably right for you. Factories make different flexes for each length of ski. Next, stand on a hard smooth surface. When you have your weight equally on both skis a sheet of paper should easily pass under the kicking area (wax pocket) of the ski. About 30 inches (75 cm) of ski should be off the ground.

When all of the weight is on one ski, the paper shouldn't be able to move. If your weight does not flatten the ski on to the snow (eliminating the bottom camber), your wax will not touch the snow and you will not be able to push forward with your power stride or when climbing. This will result in slipping and loss of power. In addition to being inefficient and frustrating, it is very tiring.

If the flex is too soft, your kicking wax will be on the snow when you are trying to glide and you will be slowed. Too soft a flex will also wear out the wax sooner. If you are more advanced and have a powerful kick, you will want a ski with a "harder flex" (more stiffness). However, less experienced skiers can generally use a softer flexed ski.

Some professional skiers, like the former Olympic gold medalist Bjorn Daehlie of Norway, uses extremely stiff skis when he is in classic races. His kick was so powerful that he could straighten the ski and get the wax pocket on to the snow, then the ski would pop back and he was certain that he won't get any drag from the kick wax in the center of the ski. Manufacturers usually categorize their skis according to ideal weight capabilities. But do your own checking. Also, if you plan to do ski touring with a backpack remember to include the weight of the pack in your calculations.

Make your final check. Once you have selected the skis which will best suit your needs, give one last check. With the ski bases together, put the tips on the floor. While holding the tail area, look along the ski to make certain that the side cuts are uniform and that the amount of flex in each ski matches. Also check to see that the bases are flat. A concave base will not ski well.

Next, with both hands grip the skis and push the bases together. Do the bases touch all along? If not, one may have a greater flex than the other. If a person can squeeze the bases together when gripping them in the middle with both hands, the flex is not too great. If they squeeze easily, the flex is probably too weak. (If you can squeeze them together with one hand they are definitely too weak.)

Boots

The original boots were the walking boots that the people of the cold North had to use to keep their feet from freezing. As shoemaking developed, regular leather boots were used. Now the boots are a lot lighter and specialized for their purpose. Be sure to get boots that are made specifically for classic cross-country skiing (although similar, there are difference between boots for classic and skate skiing).

The shoes should be comfortable and fit property, and you should try them on with the socks you would normally wear when skiing. If the boots in a given price range aren't all that comfortable, consider spending a bit more to get something that really fits well. In fact, if you're tempted to spend a little extra, it may be best to do so for the boots rather than the skis or poles.

The boots you chose will dictate the binding system you need. There are two major binding systems on the market. Although they are very similar, boots are designed to work with only one or the other. Most stores will install the binding on the skis free of charge when you buying a package.

Normal recreational touring boots are leather high-tops with various combinations of plastic, rubber or combination bottoms. The better boots are double-laced with padded tops. Some recreational boots are lined. This has some advantages relative to warmth, but they are slower to dry. The same effect can be gained from thick woolen socks.

Other types of boots are available for "non-normal" situations. For spring skiing, when the snow is more watery, a rubberized boot may be preferable, because it can keep your feet dry. For racing, a low-cut lightweight boot is the answer. For mountain skiing, other specially made boots are available — usually a cross between a downhill boot and a touring boot.

Whatever the type of boot you need, insure a proper fit. There must be adequate room for the toes, which should not be pushed against the front of the boot. The sole should be rigid enough to keep the foot directly over the ski. It should be snug enough to reduce lateral movement.

Choose the type of boot you want before you choose the binding, because most manufacturers build a boot and binding combination. One company's boot won't always fit another company's binding.

Bindings

The earliest bindings were leather thongs or pieces of twine which bound the ski to the walking boots of the early Scandinavians. As steel came into use, toe pieces were fashioned which gave the skier greater control over the ski. Now steel, aluminum or plastic gives us more control as well as greater ease in getting into and out of our bindings.

Today, bindings are somewhat standardized with a toe clip which holds the toe of the boot firm to the ski but allows the heel to lift. This allows the skier to take long strides and to move more easily uphill. But since the boot can still come fully in contact with the ski, on downhill runs the whole foot can be used for steering. To make this easier, a foot plate is part of the binding. The boot, when flat on the ski, fits into ridges on the foot plate.

From NIS skate, SNS to NNN auto bindings, there are now many different binding manufacturers and there are ski bindings for any brand of ski or boot. The store will help you find the boot and binding that match. I would start with choosing a boot that fits your foot and then the binding that goes with it.

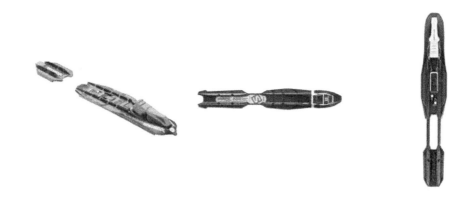

There are bindings that let you click in hands-free, as well as traditional manual bindings. Most of these bindings can be shifted forward for backward to help you find just the right balance point and stay on your feet. They are designed using strong composite materials that are made to last for many years to come.

Bindings formerly used only for racing are now the standard for all. You step into the binding, clamp it, and you are ready to ski. Because of the close tolerances of the bindings, a little snow in the gripping section can make it inoperable. So if you are standing in the snow and your bindings don't click shut easily, clean the binding bar on the front of the boot and brush out or blow out any snow in the binding.

Poles

As far as we know the original prehistoric skiers did not use poles. It wasn't until about 1500 A.D. that we find evidence of one pole being used. It apparently was used to push, stop and turn. Solid wooden poles appeared about 100 years ago, but gave way to the lighter bamboo poles. Now these have been replaced by very light synthetics — first fiberglass, now carbon or Kevlar.

Since about half of the force of propulsion comes from the upper body, the poles are extremely important. They must be strong, light and of a proper length to transmit as much horizontal force as possible. In decreasing order of strength for weight we have: Kevlar, carbon, fiberglass and other synthetics. The stiffer the pole, the more energy is transferred to the snow with the resulting forward force.

Generally poles are little longer than what was considered standard length in the past. The proper length of a pole for classical stride skiing should be to the shoulder.

Skating poles will be stiffer and longer (about 15 cm) to allow you to plant the pole behind the push-off ski. Commonly, skating poles reach to about your lower lip. Telemark skiers will use shorter poles, similar to Alpine skiers — with the length of the shaft up to the elbow and the handle coming above the elbow. While standing with your elbow at your side and your lower arm outstretched and parallel to the floor, the proper length pole will just touch the floor when you are holding it in the proper grip.

The baskets, the devices on the bottom of the poles, stop the pole tip from going deeper into the snow. Through more modern design they are also becoming lighter, but because of their placement at the end of the pole they become quite important in the speed of the pole moving forward. Softer snow requires larger baskets.

Clothing

Cross-country skiing is an aerobic activity. Upper body clothing should be in layers. Since skiers generate a great deal of heat, it is easy to perspire. The perspiration then makes them wet, and when resting, the wetness makes them cold. The trick is to take off layers of clothing as the body gets warmer, so that the heat generated by the activity is allowed to escape and the body does not become so hot that you perspire profusely. You will need a wind breaker so that you are not chilled by unexpected winds. Avoid a thick jacket unless you are Telemarking and riding the lifts.

The inner layer.

Your body will generate some moisture when you cross-country ski. The moisture will contribute to developing condensation on your clothing from the temperature difference between their warm bodies and the cold air. Wool (or synthetic base layer materials, if it is warmer) are good for drawing moisture away from your body so it can evaporate.

RaceX, Swix inner layer sweater and pant (white)

Mid Layer

This layer is for warmth and moisture absorption. Thin, warm fabrics like merino wool are good. Some skiers prefer fleece. If your mid-layer is thin and lightweight you can take it off and stuff it in your pocket or pack if you get too warm while skiing. If it's cold, it's better to add extra layers rather than wear bulky mid-layers. Extra layers are better for drawing moisture away from your body and allow you to make adjustments if conditions change.

Swix, mid layer, fleece

The outer layer

Nordic ski jackets and pants are usually constructed of windproof fabrics on the front side, and stretchy, breathable fabric on the back. The wind might blow from any direction, but when you're skiing it will almost always feel like you're skiing into the wind.

Both your pants and jacket should be constructed with front side fabrics that completely block the wind. Jackets and pants need to be well-articulated at all the joints so you can move with freedom and comfort.

Swix, Softshell jacket (blue) and Microfiber jacket (red/grey)

Softshell pant (black) and Microfiber pant (blue)

If you think you might enjoy racing, buy warm-up pants with a full-length zipper down the side of each leg. That way you can easily remove them immediately before your race begins. Unless your ski area is very rainy, you should avoid Gore-Tex and similar fabrics. They aren't breathable enough for Nordic skiing. And anything made with down or feathers is definitely not a good choice for cross-country skiing.

Hats, headbands and "necks"

When it comes to hats, it has to suit the skier. Some people prefer warm hats, while others have to wear thin hats. This has to do with perspiration and general heat production while skiing. "Buff"-style necks are often used by cross-country skiers. They seem to provide just enough warmth and protection and are easy to stuff in a pocket or clip to a drink belt. The buff can also be used as a hat or headband.

Swix, traditional hat and headband

Socks

I would advice you to wear thin socks, especially if you go fast and create a lot of heat. If your feet get cold maybe you should wear two pairs of thin socks of wool, rather than one thick pair of woolen socks.

Gloves and mittens

Mittens or gloves are generally a necessity. Your hands will stay warmer in cross country skiing than in downhill skiing — still, you never want frozen hands. Most Nordic skiers wear gloves rather than mitts because they give better control over your poles. Those of us with cold hands and poor circulation wear well-fitted Nordic ski mitts and use hand warmers as needed. We can still have pretty good control of our poles.

Eye and skin protection

Eye protection is always a concern. Both the sun and its reflection off of the snow and the irritant of the wind require good glasses or goggles. Gray or green lenses with ultraviolet ray protection are best for daytime use. Orange or yellow lenses are often better when the sun is setting. These brighter lenses help you to see better when there is no danger of ultraviolet light damage to the eyes. Sun protection is becoming ever more important as the ozone layer above us breaks up and lets in more harmful ultraviolet cancer-causing rays. Lip and face creams with high sun protective factors, preferably higher than 20, are required. Spring skiing particularly requires attention to the sun because the reflection off the snow can be brutal to your skin.

If You're Going on a Tour

If you are going for a tour, pack your knapsack with some food and drink. You should have some high-energy food. Norwegians like to make a day of skiing, so they always bring a lunch and drinks. Warm drinks are especially delicious during a long day of skiing. You should also bring a lightweight foam cushion. Sunscreen is a necessity as are lip sun blocks. Of course you will want to bring your scraper (to remove unwanted ice or wax from your skis), some waxes, and a cork to rub the wax in. Make sure that your backpack is large enough to carry all you need and still have room to store the clothes you shed as you warm up.

CHAPTER 10
Waxing and Base Preparation for Nordic Skiing

It seems that for many skiers, half of the challenge is in determining the correct wax, then waxing the skis effectively. The better wax companies spend a great deal of time and money developing and testing waxes. This has allowed them to continually improve the durability of the wax, increase the temperature range for which the wax is appropriate, and to make waxes last longer.

Swix, founded in 1946, is the leader in the field of waxing. We appreciate the assistance given in the preparation of this chapter by Harald Bjerke of Swix in Lillehammer and by his research staff. The appendix of the book has the link to the impressive manual in English for ski preparation. Swix has also made numerous videos about ski preparation and made them available for all, both in Norwegian and English.

The major obstacle for a skier to overcome is the friction of the snow — the adhesion of the snow to the base of the ski and the unevenness of the snow surface which requires that the ski "plows through" the snow. The "structure" cut into the ski base and the wax chosen increases the ability to push off with the power leg. At the same time the wax chosen for the gliding phase should reduce the friction or suction between the ski and the water under the ski. The pressure of the ski on the snow creates friction that heats and melts the snow so the skier is usually skiing on a thin coat of water. This is more prevalent during warm weather since there is more water between the particles of snow.

If you want to rank the importance of each element in terms of glide and friction, we evaluate them this way: The skis (flex, base, stiffness, etc.) are most important in terms of speed. For classical skiers the next most important factor is the kick wax. Then there is a great drop in importance to the third factor, the "structure", then last, the glide wax.

If you are a skater, there is no kick wax so the ski is far and away the most important, followed by the structure, then the glide wax. Of course, for world class racers each is very important.

Waxes are generally made from hydrocarbons, such as paraffin, mixed with other waxes. Graphite and fluorocarbons are also used in many of the newer waxes. Harder waxes are made from a mixture of the hydrocarbon waxes with other waxes of varying density. Waxes composed of larger molecules are harder than those with smaller molecules. The harder waxes will feel dry when applied. The softer waxes will feel tacky.

The harder waxes are for colder weather. The softer the wax, the more it is used for higher temperatures. Which to use? First check the outside temperature. This will give you an idea. If the temperature is over 34 degrees (1 degree Celsius), the snow will probably be wet, so a soft wax like klister is recommended. If it is less than 25 degrees (4 degrees Celsius), it should be dry so a harder wax will work. If it is between these two temperatures, try the hand test. Take a handful of snow and squeeze it. If it clumps together in a ball it is wet, it if does not compact and stays loose it is dry. The wet snow is warmer, the dry snow is colder.

Since the water content of snow varies with altitude and geographical area, the temperature range shown on the wax may not be exact for the snow on which you are skiing. The same temperature in Oslo, Mammoth, Portland or St. Paul may require slightly different waxes to give you maximum skiing performance. You may have to experiment a bit and move up or down one or two colors to get the perfect wax for your tour.

Generally it is best to wax for the coldest snow you expect. The soft wax, used for the warmer snow, will often ice up and stop sliding. So if you have used too soft a wax you may have to stop in mid-trail, clean the skis and re-wax.

You should do your waxing indoors where the ski and wax are warmer and more workable. The skis must be clean and dry for best results. It is also best to clean your skis indoors. It is preferable to clean the skis after each day's skiing. Do this by taking your plastic scraper and peeling off the excess wax. Then use a ski cleaner to finish the job. Always do a good job of cleaning before you put the skis away for the summer. If you are feeling lazy, you can leave on wax for a day or two but take off the klister!

Swix has developed a **"Wax Wizard"** where you can type in the conditions and the wizard will recommend wax products and procedures for you.

Try it out here: Swis/Wax-Resources/Wax-Wizard

Choosing the Right Wax

All the beginner needs to know is the outside air temperature, then select a wax that is appropriate for that temperature. If you are skiing the classical diagonal stride technique, you will select a kick wax and a glide wax. If you are skating, you will select only a glide wax. As you become more advanced, other factors may also be taken into consideration.

As you become more interested in top performance, you will want to know more of the "whys" and "hows" of waxing. But even as a beginner, you will want to understand why your wax is dragging or is too slippery. Was it your choice of wax or was it your technique?

Waxing is both an art and a science. And luck often plays a part, too. You may have chosen the perfect wax for the beginning of your tour, then it snowed, or the wind came up, or the sun came out — and your wax was no longer perfect.

You might say that waxing is the mental side of your skiing. It is like chess. You are playing against Mother Nature — and you won't always win. That's why skiers discuss waxing far more often than technique.

Humidity is important, but only in a general sense. If a climate is particularly dry, below 50 percent humidity, you will use one wax. If the humidity is higher than 50 percent, you can assume that the air temperature is 1 to 4 degrees higher on the Fahrenheit scale ($\frac{1}{2}$ to 2 degrees Celsius), so you will use a softer wax. If the humidity is 100 percent it is snowing!

Snow granulation

The appearance of the snow crystal and consequent snow surface is important for wax selection. Falling, or very fresh new fallen snow is the most critical situation for waxing. The sharp crystals require a wax that will resist snow crystal penetration, but at warmer temperatures must also have the ability to repel water.

Swix snow classification system

Swix has introduced a simple classification system for snow identification. The symbols are created to help skiers find the best wax for actual conditions.

1. NEW FALLEN SNOW
Below freezing

2. FINE GRAINED SNOW
Below freezing

3. OLD / GRAINED / TRANSFORMED SNOW
Below freezing

4. WET CORN SNOW
Above freezing

5. FROZEN CORN (Old) SNOW (Melted/Frozen)
Below freezing

Group 1: Falling and new fallen snow characterized by relatively sharp crystals, demanding relatively hard ski wax.

Group 2: An intermediate transformation stage, characterized by grains no longer possible to identify as the original snow-crystal shape; often called "fine-grained" snow in ski-wax terminology.

Group 3: The final stage of transformation. Uniform, rounded, bonded grains characterize the snow surface. Also called "old" snow.

Group 4: Wet snow. If snow-grains belonging to group 1, 2 or 3 are exposed to warm weather, the result is wet snow.

Group 5: Frozen or refrozen. When wet snow freezes it is identified as group 5, characterized by large grains with frozen melt water in between. The snow surface is hard and icy, normally requiring a klister as kick wax.

It is much easier to wax for old snow than for new snow. Old snow will have similar characteristics no matter where you are. But new snow varies in terms of dryness, size of flakes, and other characteristics each of which takes a different wax or technique in order to deal with the friction variations. The quality of snow also varies from area to area. So for maximum waxing effectiveness, you may have to experiment to find the very best approach to the snow you are skiing.

Heat transfer from the snow relates to both the temperature and the humidity. These factors are, of course, continually changing. If the humidity is high, there is more condensation of water on to the snow. A softer wax is therefore required. But if the air is dry, the molecules go from a solid state to gas without first becoming water, so a harder wax than the temperature would indicate should be used.

Wind is another variable in proper wax selection. The wind tends to tighten the smaller snow particles which makes more of the snow come in contact with the ski base. This increases friction. A harder (colder temperature) wax is called for.

Reflection (albedo) is an often overlooked condition. The snow can absorb energy from the sun, or on cloudy days, the heat from the earth can be reflected back by the clouds and absorbed by the snow. In either case, there can be a warming. A low angle of the sun or a cover of dry clean snow may result in almost no energy being absorbed by the snow. But a high sun or dirty or wet snow can absorb as much as 65 percent of the sun's rays.

The resultant snow friction is a combination of the above factors, plus the amount of heat generated by the friction of the ski as it passes over the snow and the unevenness of the snow (you know, when you have to plow through the trail). Temperature, of course, is a primary ingredient.

Base Preparation

Normal preparation is performed at the factory. This preparation can include either sanding or stone grinding (the preferable method). Sanding tends to rip up small strips of the base. These have to be removed at some point in order for the ski to get maximum glide. Stone grinding cuts the base and doesn't leave these fibers or "hairs."

For advanced skiers and racers, additional base preparation may be desired. You may want to do it or have a technician handle the job. In the whole world, there are only three or four top technicians with the proper equipment to do the job right. But most technicians can outperform the amateur doing the job at home. After the base preparation or "structure" is complete, you will certainly want to wax your own skis.

Structure

There is an important difference between structures produced by machine and those produced by hand. Stone ground structures are cut into the base, and are more permanent in nature. Hand structures use "imprint" tools that press the structure into the base, and consequently are temporary. Swix imprint tools have the advantage of being easy and quick to use while at the same time offer the most adaptability of adjusting the structure to match the snow type.

Structures can be classified into "fine", "medium-fine", "medium-coarse" and "coarse" structures. The most frequently used structures in World Cup are "fine" and "medium-fine". For classic races more coarse structures are used as well.

Here are two SWIXvideos of how to make structure in skis:

Links for e-book	Url- address for printed book
Press on the link (ctrl + click)	Write address into your web-browser
SWIX Structuring skis -Broken- -Structure	http://www.swixsport.com/Wax-esources/Videos-and-manuals/Cross-untry/Videos/Structuring-Broken-V-Structure
Structuring XC skis	http://www.swixsport.com/Wax-esources/Videos-and-manuals/Cross-untry/Videos/Structuring-Broken-V-Structure

SWIX SUPER RILLER *(T0401)* with 1 mm blade.

Coarse trans- formed snow		New and fine grained snow
0.25 mm	-10°C and colder	0.25 mm
0.5 mm	-5°C to -10°C	0.5 mm
0.75 mm	-2°C to -5°C	0.75 mm
1 mm	0°C to -2°C	1 mm
1 mm + 0.75 mm	0°C to +5°C	1 mm
2 mm + 1 mm	+5°C to +10°C	2 mm

Gliding wax

The basics whether you are skating or doing classical skiing, you need the right glide wax for the conditions outside. Skaters use glide wax over the whole ski because their power comes from the inside edge of the skating ski. They therefore don't need kick wax. So for skating just put glide wax over the whole ski base. Not much of a trick to that, is there? Well, maybe, because there are a number of different glide waxes. The Swix Cera Nova series is considered to be the best system in the world.

In order to develop this system with five different categories with almost 50 different waxes for gliding, a large amount of research is required. About 80 percent of the top ski racers in the world use the Swix Cera Nova system for glide waxing.

Liquid Glide

| F4 Clean & Glide Pack, 70ml | Blue Glide Liquid, 80ml | Red Glide Liquid, 80ml | Violet Glide Liquid, 80ml | F4 Glide Wax Liquid, 80ml | HVC Cold, 50ml |

Swix have divided gliding wax into different categories from 100% fluorcarbon powders, liquid or solid to 0% fluor but 100% hydrocarbon paraffine wax. There is also a product called the "Klack wolf", that is very effective on coarse grained, dirty and man-made snow. The performance and prize differs a lot between the products.

This you can read more about in the appendix and at their website:
Swix Wax and products
http://www.swixsport.com/Products/Wax-Tuning
Often, particularly for races, manmade snow is used with natural snow.
For this colder manmade snow, higher amounts of hard, brittle, synthetic paraffins are used. If the snow is warmer, less synthetic wax is used, but more fluorocarbon additives are added.

Cera Nova X

| CH6X Blue, 60g | FC4X Cera F powder, 30g | HF5BWX Black Wolf, 180g | HF10BWX Black Wolf 180g | LF7X Violet, 900g | CH6X Blue, 900g |

You can melt some wax on an old electric iron, then iron the wax on the ski. Then you scrape it off with a plastic scraper and use a cork to rub it in. You can also melt the wax in a pan and paint on a thin coat, then iron it. Always finish with brushing to make certain that the rills are able to remove the water under the base effectively. Swix also offers liquid wax as a convenient alternative to hot waxing, that is more labor intensive.

This is a general description of the methods and procedures used by servicemen on top level.

1
Scrape off the travel wax applied after the last race or training. Use the Plexi scraper (T0823D) and the groove scraper (T0088).

2
Brush with the Bronze Medium Coarse Brush (T0162) or Steel Brush (T0179). 5-10 repetitions from tip to tail, to remove remaining wax.

3
Apply the actual wax for today's conditions.
Use the iron, dripping wax on both sides of the groove.

4
The wax should easily melt. Check the temperature recommendation on the wax. Keep the iron in steady motion from tip to tail. On pass should take approx. 8-10 sec. on a skating ski.
Repeat 3 times.
Let the ski cool off 10 minutes to room temperature.

5
Don't forget to remove all excess-wax in the groove and on the sides with a scraper (T0087 or T0088). We recommend scraping the groove *before* the base to protect the surface in case the groove scraper slips and makes scratches.

6
If the actual waxes are hard, brittle like CH04X/CH06X, LF04X/LF06X or HF04X/HF06X, scrape off most of the wax before it becomes solid. After the ski has cooled off, continue scraping using a sharp Plexi scraper (T0823D).
Other waxes like CH07X/CH08X/CH10X, LF07X/ LF08X/LF10X or HF07X/HF08X/HF10X are scraped when the ski has cooled off to room temperature, 10 min.

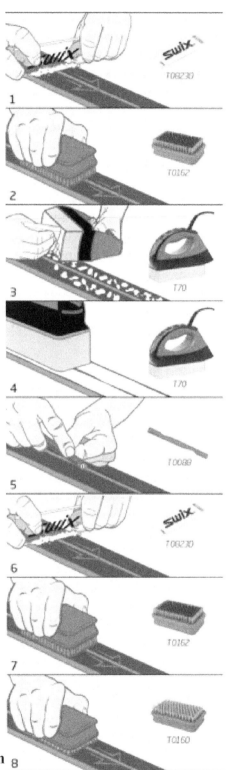

Practical application of CHX, LFX an 8

112

Sticking and Slipping

You will seldom get an absolutely perfect wax job which is ideal for the whole run. If you find yourself slipping, try a thicker coat of the same wax or a softer wax. If that doesn't work, check to see if the skis are too stiff so that the pressure of the push-off does not bend the ski allowing the wax pocket to grip the snow. Possibly your technique is poor. You could be starting the kick too late or not pushing hard enough. Another possibility is that you put kick wax over glider wax. Kick wax usually won't adhere to the harder wax.

If you find yourself sticking in the snow or have a poor glide, the wax pocket may be too long so that the kick wax slows your glide. Another possibility is that the gliding sections of your skis may need glide waxing. Your glide wax should be in the areas which touch the snow when your weight is evenly distributed on both skis. Often the bottom of the skis have picked up ice. If this is the case, scrape them fully and be sure to keep them in the snow when you ski.

Here are two SWIXvideos of how to identify the kick zone:

Links for e-ook	Url- address for printed book
Press on the link (ctrl + click)	**Write address into your web-browser**
SWIX video Kick-one-info	http://www.swixsport.com/Wax-esources/Videos-and-manuals/Cross-ountry/Videos/Kick-Zone-info
	https://www.youtube.com/watch?v=tLWjCCm-yk

About Kick Waxing in General

It is relatively simple to apply kick waxes with some experience and knowledge of the performance of the waxes you are using; however, the most experienced skier can still become confused.

In many situations, ski waxing means compromising. The final goal is superb kick and great glide; however, many times the conditions are variable and that can make this goal difficult. Most important is to find the best balance between kick and glide that will give you the best overall performance.

A common mistake is to wax too slippery. Skiers are afraid of losing glide and wax either too thin or with too hard a wax. Experience tells us that a racer will lose more time uphill, due to bad kick than gaining speed on the downhill with good glide. Swix wants to kill the myth that top-racers use slippery skis to gain better glide. Truth is that many racers apply kick waxes somewhat softer than what is suggested by temperature, create a longer kick zone and wax thicker than many recreational skiers might believe. If you look at the manual in the appendix you will get some general tips, based upon many years of field experience by the Swix World Cup service team. Following the guidelines you will get a good foundation for making waxing decisions in stressful and difficult situations.

Here is a SWIXvideo of how to apply hard grip wax:

Links for e-book	Url- address for printed book
Press on the link (ctrl + click)	**Write address into your web-browser**
How to apply gripwax	https://www.youtube.com/watch?v=tQ0Pz9axN4U

Applying and choosing hard wax

The choice of today's hard wax is based upon temperature, humidity, and snow consistency, and on your own personal experience. The temperature declarations on the boxes give a good starting point, but often you have to adjust. Apply more thin layers. By this we mean a layer, evenly distributed, without lumps. Because skis are different in stiffness, length of kick zone etc., it is difficult to give a general rule suggesting the number of layers. But normally we recommend about 4 to 10 layers. If you need fewer layers the skis are probably too soft, and if you need more layers, the skis are probably too stiff.

To avoid creating a sharp edge at the ends of the kick zone, we normally apply the hard waxes in a pyramid shape; which means that the layers gradually are applied thinner and thinner, and the wax thickness will have its peak at the highest point of the ski curvature. Normally, we apply 3-4 full length layers, and then gradually shorten the layers.

The waxing cork is an essential tool. Each layer has to be corked before applying a new one. Also, run the cork down the groove a few times (with the oval edge) to smooth the wax in this area. The closer to freezing (0°C), and the fresher the snow, the more important it is to cork the wax to an even and smooth surface, reducing the risk of icing up. For the hardest (coldest) waxes we recommend not corking too hard. A slight structure in the wax might contribute to a better kick.

After waxing: three possible scenarios

When you have finished waxing and are ready to test your skis, be prepared for one of the following three scenarios (we assume that you have applied the wax correctly length/thickness according to the stiffness of the ski and the kick zones):

A: You have correctly selected and applied the wax properly and have perfect kick.

B: You have applied too hard a wax and have slippery skis.

C: You have applied too soft a wax and the skis are icing up.

Scenario A

Congratulations and enjoy the trip!

Scenario B

If you have slippery skis, first try to apply a thicker layer of the same wax. If this does not work you probably have chosen a wax that was too hard. If this is the case then go to a wax one step softer, this may give you satisfactory kick. If you still need additional grip, continue the same way. If you feel you are getting close, more often one or two extra layers is better than going even softer.

Scenario C

In this case we are referring to snow and ice building up under the skis. By icing up there is no way out of this situation other than scraping off the warm wax and reapply a harder colder wax. The initially chosen wax was too soft and collected snow particles that were not removed by gliding. This situation usually only happens with new transformed snow. Coarse-grained snow seldom causes icing, only slow skis from using too soft a wax.

There is another type of icing. In this case there will be an almost invisible thin layer of ice on the wax, creating both slippery and slow skis. (Ice on top of snow is by no means an ideal condition). You might see some blank spots in the kick zone. If you try to put on more wax it may not work. You have to remove the ice and the ski must be dry. Then try a harder wax.

VR Waxes

VR30 Light Blue Fluor, 45g   VR40 Blue Fluor, 45g   VR45 Light Violet Fluor, 45g   VR50 Violet Fluor, 45g   VR55N Violet Fluor, 45g   VR60 Silver Fluor, 45g

About V- and VR-Waxes

Swix V-line waxes are a series of hard waxes containing somewhat less expensive raw materials than the VR-series. However, all the V-waxes are composed of the traditionally high quality Swix raw materials. The V-line waxes are still used from time to time for top-level racing, most notably the classic Swix "Blue Extra".

Application of Klisters

Swix recommends applying klister indoors; and if possible, at room temperature. Klisters are softer and much easier to handle in these conditions. Tools like a waxing table, waxing profile, waxing iron and heat gun will simplify the application and give a better final result. Always start by application of base klister.

Racing Klister

KN44 Universal Racing Klister, 55g   KX20 Green Base Klister, 55g   KX30 Blue Ice Klister, 55g   KX35 Violet Special Klister, 55g   KX40S Silver Klister, 55g   KX45 Violet Klister, 55g

How to apply klister:

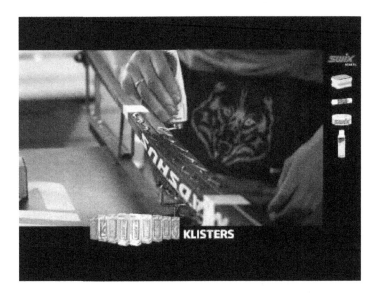

Here is a SWIXvideo of how to apply klister:

📹	
Links for e-ook	Url- address for printed book
Press on the link (ctrl + click)	Write address into your web-browser
Swix video Application- f-klister	http://www.swixsport.com/Wax-esources/Videos-and-manuals/Cross-ountry/Videos/Application-of-klister

Waxless and zero-skis

If you are overwhelmed by all the kick wax and regimes for applying this, there are skis that you do not need kick-wax. They are either zero-skis, where the kick-area is almost like sandpaper or they have a kind of "skin" in the kick-area.

If you have this type of skis you use the products listed below in the table, but first a video about waxless skis.

Here are two videos of how to take care of your zero skis:

Links for e-book	Url- address for printed book
Press on the link (ctrl + click)	**Write address into your web-browser**
Preparing zero skis	https://www.youtube.com/watch?v=zIUehqsgqMU
New-zero-skis	http://www.swixsport.com/Wax-Resources/Videos-nd-manuals/Cross-country/Videos/New-zero-skis
Refreshing zero skis	https://www.youtube.com/watch?time_continue=10&v=P-a8ler9cI

SKIN SKIS, the new waxless skis

Five years ago Atomic introduced their Skintec technology (teflon-infused synthetic mohair grip section) and since then other ski companies has been trying to improve upon the idea. Though skin skis were popular in the late 70's and early 80's, they never truly reached critical mass, primarily because ski production at the time was not quite sophisticated enough. Even my mother had skin skis, twin skin. I found them in the barn, and was surprised that this had been invented before. Now, years later, after major advances in ski construction and manufacturing technology, skins are getting more popular than traditional wax skis.

Skin skis started out as just a bridge between waxable skis and fish-scaled skis, and was marketed mostly as a racing trainer or high performance recreational ski. However, as modern skin technology continues to prove itself with flying colors, we are seeing it trickle down into more recreational skis, as well as up into high-performance race skis. In Norway the Birkebeiner has been won with skin skis.

Skin skis have an edge over traditional (or "fish scale" style) no-wax bases in two important scenarios, the first of which is icy and/or man-made snow conditions. The synthetic mohair that makes up the skin is especially good at gripping icy snow, where a traditional no-wax base might slip. Skin skis also excel in warmer snow temps when there is fresh snow, and when a dreaded "ice clump" might form on the bases of traditional skis. A third bonus is that they don't make any buzzing sound when going downhills

Zero & Waxless skis

| Skin Cleaner Pro | Zero Spray, 50ml | Zero 70 Spray, 70ml | Zero Ski Kit | Skin Care | Skin Cleaner |

Here are two videos of how to take care of your skin skis:

	🎥
Links for e-book	**Url- address for printed book**
Press on the link (ctrl + click)	**Write address into your web-browser**
Swix-skin-care	http://www.swixsport.com/Wax-Resources/Videos-nd-manuals/Cross-country/Videos/swix-skin-care
Swix-skin-products	http://www.swixsport.com/Wax-Resources/Videos-nd-manuals/Cross-country/Videos/swix-skin-products

CHAPTER 11 CONDITIONING

Skiing requires several different types of conditioning. You will need endurance conditioning to make your cardiorespiratory (heart-lung-blood) system work efficiently. You also will need endurance in the individual muscles, particularly the abdominals, the upper back, arms, hips and thighs. You will need strength to push yourself with your poles, to push off on your power stride, and to hold your body in a tuck when going downhill. And you should have a certain amount of flexibility in your joints so that you can easily go through a full range of motion. Agility and balance are also important to be able to have all of your weight on one ski while gliding.

If you just want to take some short tours, just go out and enjoy yourself. If you want to challenge yourself a bit, look over this chapter and take what you need. However, if you are a competitor and want to be the best on your high school, college, or club team you will need more. If you have aspirations to be an elite level skier, compete internationally, then win the Olympics, this chapter will be of great value—if you follow the instructions and work diligently. For the top skiers it is a year-round occupation. The question to answer is is it the most fun to glide through the forest and enjoy the freedom of being one with nature—or do you enjoy testing yourself in competition? You choose your path to joy!

Conditioning for Endurance

Cross country skiers have been shown to be the best conditioned athletes in the world in terms of cardio-respiratory endurance. The sport is therefore an ideal activity for those who want to feel fit, extend their lives, reduce heart disease and cancer risks, control their weight, and generally feel better. The benefits, of course, depend on how well trained the skier is. For someone who skis a half hour or more a day, the benefits are very good.

If you can ski every day — great! If not, you should look to other forms of endurance exercise, such as running, swimming or cycling to maintain aerobic fitness. Upon reaching the aerobic level, several changes begin to occur. More red blood cells are activated. These cells carry oxygen from the lungs to the muscles; then on the way back to the lungs, they carry carbon dioxide from the muscles to the lungs. While much of the blood is already circulating, under the demands of exercise more blood from other organs can flow into the circulatory system. The liver and spleen are particularly important in this action. Endurance activities not only energize your body and relax your mind, they help you to live longer by controlling your weight, reducing your chances for heart attacks, and releasing endorphins—those little brain chemicals that make you happy.

How Endurance Happens

Endurance develops because you will need more oxygen in your muscles for fuels. This requires your heart to beat harder and more often. After years of endurance activity your heart will enlarge functionally. (Abnormal heart enlargement can happen because of smoking, inefficient heart valves, or diseases that can damage the valves.)

Your red blood cells carry oxygen in their hemoglobin (an iron compound). You will have 20 to 30 trillion of these cells in the body. Your bone marrow makes about 2.5 million per second and they last 3 or 4 months. Most are circulating in the blood, but many are stored in your liver and spleen. Many of these are released when you exercise.

Untrained athletes often get a "second wind" after they have exercised for a few minutes. Much of the "second wind" effect is the increased number of red cells from the liver and spleen. The trained athlete already has a large number of red cells circulating, but even he or she will warm up to increase their number.

After exercising, many of these red cells remain in circulation. In a few days, however, a large number will go back to storage in the organs. But daily endurance exercise will keep most of the red cells circulating. Your body will then recognize that it needs more red cells so it will create more — if you have sufficient protein, iron, copper, vitamin B_{12} and the other ingredients necessary to manufacture the cells.

You benefit in several ways from endurance conditioning. Your body will recover more quickly following your tour, and you will be less fatigued. And since your total blood volume has increased, your body will be cleansed more quickly from all the toxic wastes which tend to build within us, even if we are active.

If a doctor were to take a red blood cell count before you began an exercise program, then take another sample after you had exercised effectively for an hour, you would find that your red cell count had increased. Since you have more red cells circulating in your blood, each teaspoon of blood will be able to carry more oxygen to the muscles and more carbon dioxide away from them.

Very simply stated this is how you provide fuel to your muscles:

- Oxygen which you breathe is attracted to the blood cells by the hemoglobin.

- Simple sugars, the simplest usable form of the food you have consumed, are added to the blood.

- From the atoms and molecules in these substances, the body's own energy sources are rebuilt.

- What remains is carbon dioxide and water. The carbon dioxide is then exhaled.

Obviously, the more red cells you have the more efficiently you can transport oxygen to the muscles and carbon dioxide away from them. This becomes even more important when you move to higher altitudes. At sea level, nearly 21 percent of air is oxygen. Almost 79 percent is nitrogen. When you exhale, almost 16 percent of your exhaled air is oxygen and about $3^1/_2$ percent is carbon dioxide.

If you were go to an altitude of 10,000 feet (3,050 meters), the amount of available oxygen drops about 30 percent. To make up for this lack of oxygen, you will breathe more often as you become acclimated to the altitude. In about a week, your red blood cells will have increased. Still, the amount of oxygen in your blood will have dropped by about 8 percent. When you come back to a lower altitude, you will have more endurance for several days because the increased number of red cells will stay with you for a while. This is why endurance athletes such as cross country skiers, marathon runners, and swimmers often train at higher altitudes.

If you have trained effectively aerobically at the lower elevations by doing aerobic dance, running, swimming, cycling, or long-distance skating, your red cells will have already increased, and you will be more ready for exercise at the higher elevation.

To improve your endurance, you must increase your heart rate significantly for at least 20 to 30 minutes. This is long enough to give you the necessary benefits to reduce heart attack risk. But if you are training for a two, three, or four-hour ski tour, you will benefit by longer workouts.

How much cardiorespiratory fitness you need is dependent on how and where you will ski. If you can walk out of your front door and put on your skis and merely want a leisurely glide through the woods, forget this program and just lace up your boots whenever you are ready. But if you want to go on a long or a fast tour, or you are going to a much higher altitude to ski, you are well advised to begin a conditioning program before your trip.

It is wise to work out at least three days a week — six is better — for six weeks. But, of course, anything is better than nothing.

As you probably know, the generally accepted standard for endurance exercise is to get your heart rate to an acceptable level for 20 to 30 minutes. That "acceptable" level is 60 to 85 percent of your maximum heart rate. And your maximum heart rate is considered to be 220 heartbeats per minute less your age. So if you are 20 years old it would be 220 minus 20 which is 200. You then work out with a pulse rate of between 130 and 170 for 20 to 30 minutes. If you are 40 years old, the calculations would be 220 - 40 = 180, so you would work out with a pulse rate of between 117 and 153. If you are 60 the figures would be 220- 60 = 160, so your target heart rate would be between 104 and 136. The higher number (the 85 percent level) is more desirable because your body will be working harder.

If you are in average condition, your resting pulse rate will be in the 70s. As you get in better shape, your resting pulse rate will drop because you will have more red blood cells working for you so your heart doesn't have to beat as often to get its work done. You can tell if you are getting in better condition by measuring your resting pulse rate. When it drops into the mid-60s, you are in better than average condition. When it gets into the 50s you are in pretty good shape. In the 40s you are in great shape. A few world class endurance athletes have pulse rates in the 20s.

To check your pulse, you can put your fingers, not the thumb, on the opposite wrist just above the thumb. Or you can put them just below your ear on the inside of the muscle on the side of your neck. Some people just like to put their hands over their hearts and feel the beat. Once you get the beat, count the number of beats in a minute. This is your pulse rate. Or you can count for 15 seconds and multiply that number by 4 to get the number of beats in a minute. If you are exercising, it is often easiest to count the beats for only 6 seconds then multiply that number by 10 to get your pulse rate during exercise.

Before you start an exercise program, it is always a good idea to have a physical examination. This will give you your blood pressure, your cholesterol levels, your red blood cell count, the condition of your heart and a number of other important indicators.

In the Melbourne Summer Olympics, a Norwegian won the 800 meter run. As part of his training for the Olympics he decided to workout with the Norwegian cross country ski team. They were going to run up a steep mountain ten times. He managed only three climbs.

VO2 max

The VO$_2$max is the measure of how much oxygen a body can use in a given period of time. The untrained male averages 35 to 40 kilograms of oxygen per minute. Untrained females are in the 27 to 31 range. These scores can be increased with effective endurance training and they will reduce as we age.

Athletes who compete in endurance sports like cross country skiing, swimming, long distance cycling, marathon running, and rowing will have higher scores. Athletes in American football, baseball, or gymnastics will be closer to the untrained person. Elite male distance runners are often in the 85 range and female runners in the 77 range. *Tour de France* winners may be as high as 88. The Norwegian multiple Olympic and World Champion skier, Bjorn Daehlie, measured a phenomenal 96 in the pre-season, and Norwegian cyclist Oskar Svendsen measured 97.5 when he was 18. The Norwegian physiologist who measured Daehlie believed that Bjorn could top 100 during a race.

A recently released study of Norwegian Nordic skiers (cross country, biathlon—ski shooting, combined (combination of ski jumping and cross country skiing) showed that the average for males was 84.3 and for females 72.6. International medal winners were higher, as might be expected.

The VO$_2$ max is a major factor in skiing effectively for long distances, but your skiing efficiency and the efficiency of your skis are also factors.

Off-Season Conditioning

In the off-season, the summer and fall, swimming (especially the crawl or the back stroke) will not only help to maintain your aerobic level in the cardio-respiratory system, but it will develop more of the slow-twitch fibers in the upper back (latissimus dorsi) and the back of the arms (triceps). This development should help your arms for poling next season. On the other hand, skating, running or cycling should help to develop muscles in the legs.

For these reasons, many people do "cross training" in the off-season. This may include two or three days of running, cycling, skating, roller-skiing or working on a cross country ski machine (such as NordicTrack) for the lower body and two or three days of swimming, rowing or paddling for the upper body. This can reduce any boredom you might experience merely running, skating, or roller skiing. But if you are intent on being the best trained skier you can be, stick with the roller skiing and running. Do a lot of uphill work

Another exercise, which will condition your legs, can be done while you watch TV. Put five or six books on the floor in a stack. Start with both feet on one side of the books then jump to the other side, landing on both feet. Continue to jump back and forth without stopping until next December or until the first snow falls. Boy, will you be in great shape for the season! Jumping rope is another exercise which will condition both your heart and your legs.

Any exercise that gets your heart beating fast enough to get into your target zone is good. Cross country skiing, swimming, running, cycling — even sex. Just remember that whatever you are doing, get to your target rate and stay there for at least 20 minutes. Thirty is better. Also you should warm up before you hit your target range. So just perform your activity at a little slower pace for a few minutes before you speed up and hit your target rate. Then at the end of your exercise, cool down by slowing your exercise and letting your heart rate drop. Then finish with some stretching. Some people like to stretch before their aerobic workout. That's OK. Just do some aerobic warm-up, such as jogging or skiing; stretch; get into your real aerobic workout; then stretch again. The stretching after the workout is more important than that done before the workout.

Developing Muscular Endurance

It's not enough to have a healthy heart and lots of red blood cells. Individual muscles also have to have specific endurance. Muscles used in an endurance activity will develop a better capacity to use the oxygen and sugars which the blood brings to them. There will be more hemoglobin in the muscles, more readily available fuel, and there may even be a different type of muscle tissue developed.

There are three different types of muscle fibers, the slow-twitch (red or type I), the intermediate (type II a), and the fast-twitch (white or type II b). The fast-twitch fibers contract quickly, but cannot endure many repetitions. Olympic weight lifters have a high percentage of these because they need only one powerful contraction, then they rest for many minutes. Endurance athletes, such as cross country skiers, swimmers and distance runners have a large percentage of the slow-twitch fibers. These fibers contain more fuel and can contract many times.

Research indicates that the type of training a person does can change the type of fibers present. It may be that it is the intermediate fibers which change more toward the fast- or the slow-twitch (type II) fiber. Trained cross country skiers have 70 to 80% of their muscle fibers as the slow twitch (type II) variety. Marathon runners are more likely to be over 80 percent. It would seem then that appropriate aerobic training should result in more effective muscles and better muscular endurance.

Muscular endurance and muscular strength are at opposite ends of the spectrum. Strength is how much force you can generate in one muscular contraction, while endurance is how long you can continue muscular contractions with relatively little resistance against them. In Nordic skiing you never need the maximum force that an Olympic weight lifter would need. But there are times when you need more than the normal amount of force, such as in climbing hills. Your strength is determined primarily by the number of individual muscle fibers you have contracting in one contraction. No one can contract all of the muscle fibers in a muscle at the same time. Few people can even contract 50 percent of their muscle fibers at one time. So your strength training program is designed to teach your brain to be able to contract more muscle fibers at one time. Strength can greatly increase the force exerted by your power ski and by your poling action. This, in turn, will increase your glide and your stride distance.

Some Principles of Exercise training

1. Your body should be in the same posture in the fitness room as it will be in your activity.

2. Exercise your muscles to exhaustion.

3. Strength, strength endurance, and cardiopulmonary endurance are highly specific in their requirements.

4. Your body should have a general amount of strength in every muscle group, and be particularly strong on the core muscles in the abdominal area.

Now let us go more deeply into each of these principles.

1. For many years, we have believed that any exercise that strengthens the muscle will be effectively used in the activity. We now know that this is not entirely true. Strength is strongly dependent on the posture that the exerciser is in while during the exercise. So a freestyle swimmer should do exercises in the prone position, the backstroker should do them in a supine position, and the skier should be doing them in an upright position. It appears that since the brain is the major stimulator of muscles, the position of the head is important in signaling which and how many muscle fibers to use.

This was found by Dr. Larry Morehouse of UCLA in 1957, but nobody paid attention to it. In fact strength training for college athletes was forbidden at this time because of a fear of "muscle-boundness." It was not until the 1970s, when the University of Nebraska football team began strength training, which translated into many championships, that the other colleges adopted strength training for their football teams. Eventually it worked into track and field, basketball, gymnastics, and eventually into golf and skiing.

The last major researcher to find the same thing was Dr. Greg Wilson. He had been second in the world in powerlifting and was a professor of sport science in Australia. He then took a position as weight lifting coach in Indonesia. In his 8 years of coaching in two Olympics, his lifters won 9 Olympic medals. So he has performed: as a champion athlete, an incredibly successful coach, and while a professor, as the most respected and creative researcher in strength training in the world.

In his last study he had people doing bench presses, throwing a bar upward from a supine position, sitting with the back against the wall and throwing a medicine ball as far as possible, and doing push-ups. The identical muscles are used in all of these actions-- the upper chest and triceps primarily. He found no transference of strength between the activities. Morehouse found the same, as did Dr. Sam Britton of California State University at Northridge. And those who have done similar studies have found the same, that there is no significant transfer of strength between the exercises. The realities are that many of the strength trainers are either former Olympic lifters or former power lifters. They do have knowledge of gaining strength, but seldom utilize this important factor.

2. The body adjusts to stress. When we are too warm, we perspire. When we run a long way, more red blood cells are put into circulation. When we exercise some muscle group to exhaustion, the brain learns to contract more fibers and one time and the muscle fibers often will increase in size.

3. If you are trying to win the Olympics in weightlifting, you need to exhaust your muscles in one or a few repetitions. If you are a long-distance swimmer or a cross-country skier, you will want exhaustion to occur after many

hundreds or thousands of repetitions. This is also true in cross country skiing. But climbing steep hills requires muscular strength as well as muscular endurance.

4. Your body should have good general body strength, especially in the core (the abdominal and lower back areas). However, having a skier or swimmer do standing presses to exhaustion is generally a waste of time. The same is true of squats. While a swimmer needs leg strength to push off the wall and the dive for a turn, the pushoff is not straight up as in a squat. So, it should be done in a prone position. But all of a skier's strength and endurance are needed in an upright position, so all exercises should be done upright. So if you wanted effective pushing strength, for some reason, use a sitting shoulder press machine rather than doing bench presses lying supine on a bench.

What Has This Got To Do With Skiing?

While cross country skiers need good core strength endurance, the major muscle groups that they will use when skiing are the hip extensors and the shoulder extensors. If a skier gets tired in any other area than the hips and shoulders, additional exercises must be prescribed.

For the hip extensors (primarily the gluteals and the hamstrings) the NordicTrack machine (illustrated) will work both the hip and shoulder extensors for endurance conditioning. However, it may not offer enough maximum resistance to effectively increase the muscular endurance and muscular strength needed for uphill racing. Similarly, the shoulder muscles (latissimus dorsi and triceps, primarily) may also not be sufficiently challenged for the hard poling required uphill and at the end of a race.

A pulley machine with a stack of pin select weights can be used effectively for both hip and shoulder extensions.

There are a number of dual pulley adjustable pin-select weight machines on the market. Most have the pulleys too wide for optimal skiing conditioning needs. The ideal is to have the pulleys about shoulder width apart. They can then be used for both shoulder and hip exercises. For the shoulder hyperextensions, set the pulley about a foot above the head (30 cm). For the leg exercises (hip hyperextensions) set the pulley about a foot (30 cm) from the floor.

This illustration shows the hip hyperextension that is critical for skiers. There are no machines currently available for skiers to do their hip hyperextensions with alternating legs—which would be the ideal. (A dedicated competitive skier might construct a stable seating post high enough so the feet do not touch the floor while doing alternate hip hyperextensions. If you are interested, contact the publisher at totalhealthpublications@gmail.com to discuss the project with the author.)

Generally skiers will have to work one leg at a time.

The best strength endurance program for highly competitive skiers is starting at a one repetition maximum (the most weight you can lift one time), try a second reputation, if the machine will not budge, have a partner move the pin to the next lightest weight and do as many repetitions as possible. The partner then moves the pin to the next lightest weight and the exerciser does as many repetitions as possible. This is continued until a total of at least 200 repetitions are completed. (This would be a type of reverse pyramid program.) The partner notes the weight and the number of repetitions completed at each weight. This progress card is used every workout. There should be as little rest as possible at each new weight. As the exerciser gets to the lower weights he or she may be able to do more than 20 repetitions. If so, the partner moves the pin to the next highest weight.

Because of the machines available, skiers must usually use a typical dual pulley machine using an ankle strap for the leg work. because of the limitation of the current machines, each leg will have to be exercised independently. The ideal would be to have a NordicTrack type machine with a weight stack, rather than the magnetic wheel that provides resistance in the NordicTrack.

This difficult strength and endurance leg workout should only be done about every four days to give the muscles time to recover. If the skier does only classical skiing, the foot should be pointed forward throughout the exercise. But if the skier also does skating, every other workout should be done with the toes pointed outward at a 45° angle. So the classical stride would be one worked out, four days later the skating workout, then four days later the classical work.

The same is true with the shoulder work. However, since shoulders may not be able to take the continuous pressure as easily as the hips can, you should be aware of pain in the shoulder joint and rest it if necessary. The shoulder workouts should all be spaced four days apart. So the competitive skier can do hip extension one day, rest one day, then shoulder extension the next day. The correct term for extending the leg behind the torso is called hyperextension. The same term is used when the arms are extended backward past the torso.

Just as the foot has its angle differently for skating and classical skiing, the arms are called upon to do different tasks when skiing. So, one workout will have the skier alternating the arms as in traditional classic skiing, then four days later both arms will be hyperextended simultaneously in the workout.

The arc of the leg should be from about a 30 degree forward flex to about 45 degrees of hyperextension. For the arms, start at 90 degrees or more of forward flexion to about 30 degrees of hyperextension. Studies have shown that most athletes gain strength primarily through the arc that is involved in the exercise. Some people will gain strength in more degrees than the arc of the exercise, but to be safe, exercise through the whole arc that you use in competition.

So, for the highly competitive skier, the off-season weight program would be: hip hyperextension for classical skiing, rest one day, alternating arm hyperextensions, rest one day, skating hip hyperextensions with the toes turned out 45°, one day rest, double arm shoulder hyperextension's, rest one day, etc. To keep the strength endurance gained in the off-season, do a set of arm and leg

The endurance work will be skiing in the winter and roller skiing or skating or running in the summer.

5. The general strength program would include abdominal, lower back, quadriceps, have squats, biceps, triceps, upper and lower chest, etc. (For an outstanding book on strength training we recommend: Strength Training by Wells and O'Day.)

Understanding Muscles

The Parts of a Muscle

The muscle belly is made up of large numbers of fasciculi (generally containing 100 to 150 individual muscle fibers). The average biceps muscle contains about 100,000 such elements.

The individual fibers vary in length from 1 to 40 millimeters (mm) about 0.04 to 1.6 inches in length and 10 to 100 micrometers (a micrometer is a millionth of a meter, or 0.00004 of an inch) in diameter.

Each individual fiber is made up of slender threads called myofibrils. Each myofibril is about as long as the muscle fiber but only about 1 to 2 micrometers in diameter.

Each myofibril is made up of a number of sarcomeres. These are the parts of the fiber which actually shorten. (They are about 2 micrometers long.)

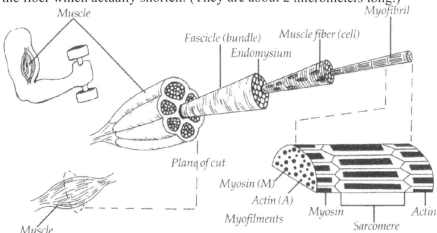

The myofibrils are made up of still smaller segments called myofilaments. There are over 1,000 of these in each sarcomere.

These cells and parts of cells are made from amino acids which form the protein that is a major building block of each cell. About 20% of a muscle is made of protein (amino acids), about 75% is water and the remaining 5% is made up of other things such as salts, phosphates, and minerals. The amino acids are formed according to directions sent by the DNA (deoxyribonucleic acid) genes in the chromosomes of the cells of the muscles.

Within the sarcomere are the fibers which produce the contraction. While we don't know exactly how a muscle cell contracts, there are some theories. Since the threads creating the contractions are about 5 to 15 millionths of a meter long (about one ten-millionths of an inch) and a diameter which is much smaller. With such tiny parts of the muscle it is a wonder that we know anything at all!

The parts of the muscles that do the contracting are the actin and myosin in the sarcomere. The far ends of the two actin bands are attached to Z lines. During a contraction the two actin bands are pulled across the myosin band. This pulls the Z lines closer together so the sarcomere shortens. With hundreds or thousands of sarcomeres similarly contracting simultaneously, the muscle shortens. The following diagrams illustrate this action. The arrows illustrate the "crossbridges" that pull the actin across the myosin.

Normal muscle ready to contract

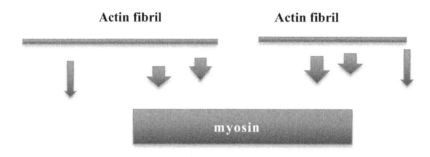

A stretched muscle fiber can result in fewer cross bridges so there is less potential strength

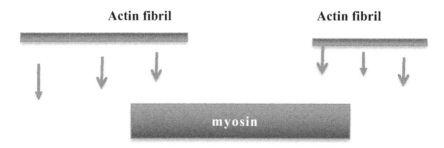

ges connecting the actin and myosin so there is more potential force in the sarcomere).

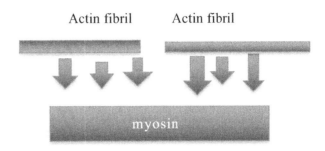

The actin fiber looks like a double strand of beads which are twisted. The myosin has outcroppings from its body which seem to grip the sides of the actin "beads" to slide the actin along the side of the myosin.

Not all of the fibers in a muscle will contract at the same time, but every fiber contracting will do so to its maximum ability. This is known as the "all or none" principle. The greater percentage of fibers that a person can make contract at one time, the greater the force the muscle exerts.

When contracting the sarcomere can shorten by 20%-50%. This contraction begins by the reception of a nerve impulse. That impulse requires that there be sufficient fuel in the cell to make the contraction. That fuel is called ATP (adenosine triphosphate). As one phosphate is broken off from the larger ATP molecule energy is produced. We don't have an unlimited amount of ATP, so the phosphate has to be replaced. This is done by taking the phosphate from creatine phosphate (CP) which is also in the muscle.

There is generally three to five times more CP in the muscle than ATP, so it makes an efficient molecule to resynthesize the ATP. Some people supplement their diets with creatine phosphates to help in this action. This type of energy production can last only a few seconds before the fuels are exhausted. This is called anaerobic activity and is the type of muscle fueling which is found in heavy weight lifting or in short sprinting.

If the activity is to last more than several seconds, energy from glycogen (sugars) and oxygen must be used to resynthesize the ATP. This is called aerobic (with air) exercise. This begins when you take your first breath during exercise so the oxygen begins to aid in the resynthesis of the ATP in well under a minute. Endurance exercise, like cross country skiing, makes this system more efficient.

Increasing Your Strength

First, let's take a look at the body's musculature to understand where the skier needs strength and strength endurance.

Major Anterior Muscles

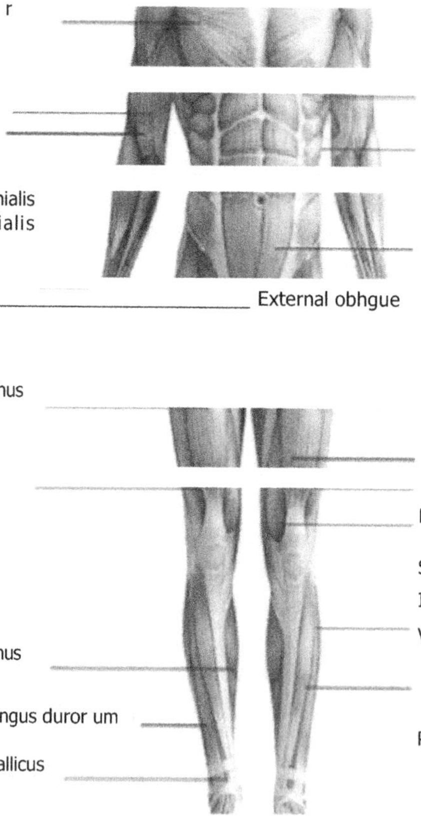

5ternocleidomastoic

Deltold

P e c t o r

a l i s

major

Teres major

Coracobrachialis
brachialis

Serratus antenor

Brachbradialis _____ External obhgue

Rectus abdomlnis

Gluteus mechus

Ihopsoas

Pechreus

Tensor fasciae latae

Rectus remoris

Sartonus

I h o t b a l   b a n d

Vastus medialts

Gastrocnennus

Extensor longus duror um

Extensor hallicus

Peroneus longus

1

Skiing is a
power activity with the power coming from muscles on the backside of the body.
However, pulling the leg forward on each stride you need

Tibialis antenor

133

the abdominals, quadriceps (muscles in the front of the hips and thighs. Lifting the poles forward is done with the biceps and deltoids primarily.

Major Posterior Muscles

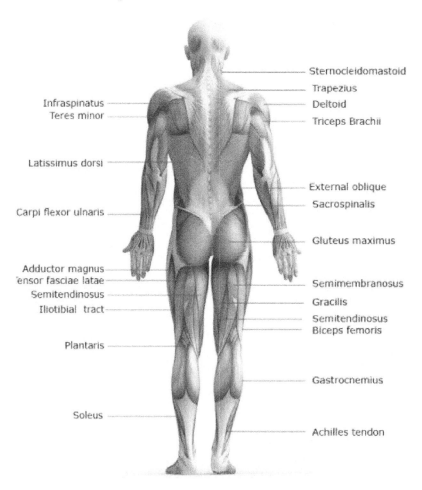

The leg power comes from the muscles in the buttocks and the muscles on the back of the thigh. Pole power comes from the latissimus dorsi and the triceps. The trapezius both stabilizes the shoulder and aids in the pole push.

The following exercises will help you to condition your muscles. If you are trying to get stronger, exhaust your muscles in less than 10 repetitions. Exhaustion in one to three repetitions is best. But if you are working on developing muscular endurance, such as you will use in cross country skiing, do a number of repetitions. A good range for most people would be 25 to 200. (See reverse pyramid program above.) But remember that your muscles should be exhausted when you finish. You know you're exhausted when you can no longer eke out one more repetition. It is only by getting your muscles very tired that will get you the best results. However, keep in mind that anything is better than nothing.

Strength Exercises for the Abdomen

The Abdominal Curl: Everyone knows this exercise but some have not kept up with the latest techniques to make it more effective. Lie on the floor or on your bed:

1) Put your hands on your chest (to avoid pulling in on the neck muscles).

2) Bring your feet up as close to your hips as possible (so that you don't use the small hip flexing muscles which attach to the lower back — especially important for women).

3) Look at the ceiling and continue looking at the same spot during the exercise (so that you don't stretch the muscles in the back of your neck).

4) Raise your shoulders and concentrate on bringing the lower part of your ribs closer to the top of your hips.

5) Do as many repetitions as you can because you want muscular endurance from these muscles.

This exercise strengthens the abdominal muscles which will begin your poling action. As you start to pole, you will use these muscles as you bend forward at the waist.

There are actually four sets of muscles in the abdominal wall. One, the rectus abdominis, does most of the work in the curl or sit-up. There are two sets of angled muscles called the obliques. These assist in the sit-up but also work in twisting and side bending actions. The following exercises work the obliques.

As you become stronger you should be able to do the "crunch." In this exercise the neck, upper back and hips are lifted from the floor.

Crunch

The Twisting Abdominal Curl is the same as the curl exercise, but as you raise your shoulders you bring your right shoulder toward your left knee on one repetition, then your left shoulder to your right knee on the next one.

If you belong to a gym, there may be a rotary abdominal machine which is more effective than the twisting sit-up. Or you can work with a partner. While sitting in a chair holding a rod (broom, pipe, etc.) across your upper chest, have your partner give resistance to one end of the rod while you twist against it.

Rotational abdominal with partner

Another exercise which can develop the abdominal obliques is \ the side situp. Put your feet under a sofa or have someone hold them down; then, while on your side bring your shoulders and torso upward.

Side Sit-up

Strength Exercises for the Shoulders and Arms

Shoulder Extension is the most important exercise for cross country skiers to do unless they have been swimmers or gymnasts. The upper back, latissimus dorsi, and back of the arm muscles, triceps, are not used as often in other sports, but contribute much of the power to the poles.

Sitting Shoulder Extension (Straight Arm Pull-down)

If you belong to a gym use a pull-down pulley, and pull it down with your arms straight.

If you don't belong to a gym, you can buy stretching bands at a sporting goods store or surgical tubing (about 8 to 10 feet) from a pharmacy. Screw an eye bolt into a door jamb or into a wall in the garage; anchor the middle of the band to the bolt. Tie knots in the end of the tubes, or make a handle, then pull — alternating arms or using both arms together. You want to use your muscles through the same range of movement you will use in skiing, so pull from a spot directly in front of your shoulders to as far back as you can pull.

Using dumbbells, you can bend forward at the waist, then alternately bring your right arm as far back as you can, then do the same with the left arm. You can also lie on your back with your arms on the floor behind your head. With dumbbells, bricks or books, bring your arms forward until they are vertical over your head.

Another way to develop these muscles is with a partner. Take two lengths of rope or two poles at least six feet long. Face each other. Each holds one end of each pole and pulls back with his or her right arm while resisting each other with the left arms. Then both pull with arms while they resist each other with their right arms.

The pull and the resisting are working the lats and one of the three heads of the triceps. While doing this exercise keep the arms straight — no bend at the elbows.

The triceps (three heads) straighten (extend) the elbow. One of the three heads crosses the shoulder joint so it works with the lats in pulling the upper arm backwards. All three heads work to straighten the arm at the elbow joint. This is done in the last part of the poling action.

Tricep Extensions — Machine

Tricep Extensions — Dumbbells

If you belong to a gym, use the triceps extension machine or do triceps extensions on the tat pull-down machine. You can also lift dumbbells over your head. If you don't belong to a gym, you can do push-ups with either your feet or your knees on the floor.

Strength Exercises for the Legs, Hips and Knees

The front of the thigh or quadriceps hold you in a tuck position when you are gliding on one leg, and they bring your legs forward as they recover from the push or "kick."

If you are in a gym, use the quadriceps machine. If not, get a partner. Sit on a table and have your partner place both hands on your ankle and give resistance. Straighten your leg. If you don't have a partner, you can use that same rubber band which was recommended for the upper back.

Quadriceps — Manual

Quadriceps—Machine

The back of the thigh or hamstrings provide much of the push backward when skiing. Gyms have special machines for the hamstrings. If you don't have access to a machine, get your trusty old partner, lie face down on the floor or a table, and have your partner push against your ankle as you lift your lower leg from the floor. Keep your knee on the floor or table.

To get the upper part of the rear of the hips, the muscles that do most of the pushing work in your skiing, lie on a table face down with your hips on the table with your thighs past the table and your toes touching the floor. You can use a partner if you want more strength, or do it alone if you want more endurance by doing many repetitions. Start with one toe touching the floor while the other leg is brought as high as possible, then alternate legs. This will look like an exaggerated kicking action for a person swimming the crawl stroke. Another partner exercise for hip extension is mentioned under the hip flexion exercise.

Hamstring Exercise (Leg Curl)

Fitness rooms all have either squat racks or other machines which allow you to extend your legs. But it can be done easily at home. You can just do a three-quarter knee bend (don't bend your knees more than 90 degrees), or you can do half knee bends if you want twice the amount of resistance. To do a half knee bend, hold a table top to steady yourself. Using only one leg, bend down 45 to 90 degrees then return to a standing position. By doing it on only one leg, you get the same effect as doing it with two legs while holding a barbell equal to your own weight.

You can also do an isometric contraction (bend partway down, then hold without moving). This would be the position you would take in skiing downhill fast—the "egg" position is used to reduce air resistance that will slow the skier. If you are unsure of your strength, do the exercise from a chair.

Hip and Knee Extensions — Squat

Hip abductors move your legs sideways away from the midline of your body. They are very important in helping you to maintain balance. When shifting your weight to the new gliding ski, it is the abductors, those muscles on the outside of your lower hip, which stop your motion outward and allow you to catch your balance. They are also involved in the pushing action of a skater.

Hip Abductors — Multi-hip Machine

Some gyms have special machines for the abductors. If there is a "multi-hip" machine, use it. Most gyms have low pulley weights with anlde straps. Stand with one side of your body next to the machine, and put the ankle strap on the leg farthest from the machine. Lift the leg sideways keeping it straight.

With a partner, lie on your side. Let your partner put pressure on your knee or ankle, then lift your leg as high as you can. If you have no partner, you can do the same exercise alone — you just won't get as strong, but you can get just as much endurance. You can also do it yourself by sitting with your knees close to your chest, then give pressure with your hands to the outside of your knees as you bring your knees outward.

You can also use the rubber bands. Attach one to a low part of a wall, hook your foot into a loop on the end of the band and lift your leg outward.

Hip adductors are those muscles high on the inside of your thighs. They bring your legs back together if they have been moved outward by the abductors. The exercises are just the reverse of those for the abductors.

If your gym has a machine, use it. If there is a low pulley station, stand sideways to the pulley but a yard away from the machine. Put the strap on the ankle nearest the machine. Let your leg move outward (toward the machine) with the weight, then bring it back to the other leg.

With a partner lie on your back. Spread your legs. Let your partner give pressure inside your ankles. Bring your legs back together. If you wish, you can combine the adductor and abductor muscles in this exercise. While lying on your back, your partner will give you hand pressure on the outside of both ankles. You will spread your legs against the pressure (abductors). Then your partner will give you re on the inside of your ankles, and you will bring your legs back together (adductors).

Without a partner just sit on the floor with your feet about 12 inches from your hips and the heels together. Spread your knees outward, then grasp the inside of your knees with your hands. Bring your knees together as you resist the movement with your hands. You will feel the tension inside your upper thighs.

Hip flexion exercises help you to quickly bring the ski forward after the power phase. It can be done on a multi-hip machine or with a partner. If you have a partner you can lie on your right side. With your left leg back, as if you have just finished a long stride, have your partner put pressure on the front of your ankle, then bring your leg as far forward as you can. The farther forward you go the less power you will have, so your partner will need to apply less pressure as you move your leg forward.

Once the leg is forward, your partner can put pressure on the back of your heel, then you can swing your leg back as far as it will go. This is hip extension.

Hip extension exercises can be done on machines or with a partner. These are muscles that power your ski push off.

Hip hyperextension on multi-hip machine

Hip hyperextension with partner

Thigh rotation develops the muscles which move your ski tips in or out. This action is done high in the hips. Sit on the floor with your legs stretched out. Turn your feet inward as far as they can go and hold. Then twist outward — and hold. It is more effective if a partner can give your feet resistance in each direction.

Exercises for the Lower Back

Lower back exercises should be geared to muscular endurance more than strength, so you will want many repetitions. You can lie on the floor face down and lift your shoulders about six inches from the floor then return to the floor. (You don't want to go too high with your shoulders because you don't want to create a "sway back" in your exercise.)

You can also do this with a partner. With the partner holding your legs, and your hips and legs on a table, bend forward at the waist to 60 or 90 degrees then lift your torso back up so that it is in line with your legs and hips. Again, you don't want to arch your back during the exercise.

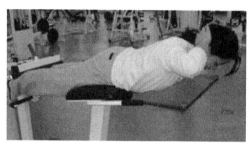

Lower Back — arches

Repetitions and Weight

How many reps and how much weight you use depends on your goals. For pure strength, you should be exhausted in one to three repetitions. But pure strength is not what you want for skiing. You want a certain amount of strength and you want muscular endurance. Aim for between 20 to more than 100 repetitions. You may have to work up to 20 reps from just a few reps. Don't be discouraged. Anything you do will help.

Using "manual resistance" with a partner can actually be better than using weights. Your partner can adjust the pressure to make you work to a maximum level on each repetition. Weights can't do this. Only partners and "isokinetic" machines have this capability. So, if you are using a partner, don't figure you are not getting the best strength workout. In fact, that partner is probably entitled to a good dinner once a week for helping you to develop your "habit."

If you are a racer and one group of muscles needs more conditioning, a reverse pyramid workout is suggested. For this you will need a weight machine.

Start at the level where you can do only one repetition. Do it. Try another. Then decrease the weight and repeat the exercise. Continue this, exercising to exhaustion at every step, until you have done a total of 200 repetitions. This is only for the highly dedicated racer and should only be done for one or two muscle groups at each workout.

Becoming More Flexible

Flexibility comes from stretching the body's connective tissue — the tissue that holds one bone to another (ligaments), the tissue that holds

144

muscles to bones (tendons) and the tissue which holds the individual muscle bundles together. If you are not flexible, you will not have a full range of motion for each joint. When you are too tight, you must use excess muscle power just to make a simple movement.

For example, if the connective tissue in the front of your hips is too tight, you won't be able to extend your ski as far backward in your power stroke. If the connective tissue in the front of the shoulders is too tight you won't be able to push back as far with your poles. Also, if you are not sufficiently flexible, it is easier to sprain (ligament damage) or strain (muscular or tendon damage).

Flexibility is quite simple to achieve. Most of us touched our toes every day during physical education classes in school, but we may have forgotten to continue the practice. You could probably easily touch your toes when you were 12. Can you do it now? The connective tissue tends to shorten if we do not keep it stretched, so most of us have lost some flexibility between the time we were in the eighth grade and now. So we need to get back into some of our childhood habits.

Stretches should be held for 20 to 30 seconds in order to get the maximum benefits. If you find that you are particularly tight in one area, do the exercise several times a day.

Stretching should be done at the end of a workout when the muscles and tendons are warm.

Some Principles Regarding Stretching

1. Not all joints need to be stretched to the maximum—over-stretching can set up joints for injury. Bending the knee past 90 degrees is approaching the point where the knee ligaments can be stretched. This weakens the structure of the knee.

➤ Ligaments are connective tissues that hold bone to bone and when stretched weaken the joint structure. When overstretched it is called a sprain. Sprained ligaments shorten slowly. That why sprained joints, like ankles, are often re-sprained.

➤ Tendons are connective tissues that attach muscles to bones. When overstretched it is called a strain.

➤ Muscles are more easily stretched, but can be overstretched. This, too, is called a strain. But it may also be called a "pull."

2. Some joints can be weakened by improper exercises—like deep knee bends (squats), back hyperextensions, excessive neck flexion, etc. What is good for a yogi is not necessarily good for a skier!

3. Nine out of ten people should not do passive stretching (the typical stretching exercises) before a workout or a race. The stretching can

separate the actin and myosin fibrils too far and muscle is weakened. (See section on muscles above.) Because the actin elements are farther apart they can be more easily pulled completely away from the myosin. If this happens to many sarcomeres at the same time you have a muscle strain. Studies have shown more injuries and less muscle power in muscles that have been passively stretched before a competition. Stretching also signals the muscle to relax, so the athlete feels better.

4. The one in ten who profits from pre-competition stretching is the athlete with "stiff" muscle—where the actin elements are too close together to allow an effective full contraction.

5. Pre-workout and pre-competition warmup, skiing slow, then fast, will give the dynamic stretching needed for the muscles and tendons.

6. Passive stretching is important so that the skier is not using extra energy to overcome tight connective tissue. For example, when the leg is brought forward in the stride, if the gluteals and hamstrings are tight, extra energy will be required to overcome that tightness and the forward movement may be slightly slowed.

Here are some stretches that may be done after a workout or competition.

Lower Back and Hamstrings

Toe Touch

The Toe Touch keeps your lower back and the back of your hips and thighs flexible. While most people do it standing, it is more effective to do it Sitting on the floor. When you are sitting and stretching forward, the muscles in the back of your torso and thighs relax so you can stretch farther. When you are standing,

those same muscles remain somewhat tight because they are
fighting the gravity which is allowing you to bend downward.

The leg straddle stretches the tissue of the upper inner thighs. This
allows you to spread your legs more easily in a sideways movement such
as when doing the wedge or skating. While standing, move your feet
sideways wiggling them farther and farther out each day.

The lunge is a forward-backward stretch for the tissue at the front and
the rear of the upper thighs. Becoming flexible in these areas makes it easier
to do any striding or skating and allows an effortless reach for the glide. Put
the right foot forward and the left back. Keep moving them farther and farther
apart. Then put the left leg forward and the right back.

Lunge

Trunk twists stretch the middle of your torso. You will want to be
flexible in this area, especially for classic skiing. You can stretch from the
sitting position or the standing position.

The front of the shoulder stretch also allows you to push farther back
with your arms in the poling action. While standing with your arms at your
side, bring both arms directly backward as far as you can — and hold.

But stretching for skiing can be overdone!

Oops! More flexibility than you need on the trail!

Training for Agility and Balance

You are already well aware that skiing is a balance sport along with its endurance requirements. Skiing technique is all about balance in motion. Just think about all of the internal and external factors that must be balanced and counterbalanced to skate and glide or to ski down a difficult run. You've got the steepness of the slope, the depth and density of the snow, the texture of the snow and the visibility, all of which vary from turn to turn. In order to skillfully ski through all this, you've got to be balanced on one ski most of the time. When turning you must guide them left and right in order to regulate your speed and momentum. Indeed, high-level skiing requires an unbelievable sense of balance and equilibrium.

You cannot get enough work on balance, on or off the snow. When you balance you are training your brain. It must continually make adjustments in your muscle contractions to keep you from falling right or left, forward or backward. If you are standing on one leg, your balance forward and backward is easy to find, because your foot is longer than it is wide so your forward-backward balance is easier than your side-to-side balance. If you put on skis, this difference is emphasized because the ski is longer than your foot and also narrower than most feet. And it is more slippery than your foot bottoms.

So while forward-backward balance is essential, it is much easier to achieve than side-to-side balance. Add to this the fact that while skiing, you shift your weight from one ski to the other quickly. If you are standing on a floor on two feet then slowly shift your weight to one foot, it is difficult enough to balance. But when you jump to one foot and try to hold a balanced position before hopping back to the other foot, it is much more difficult. It is this dynamic shifting of balance thousands of times during a tour which is the key to technique.

Balance Exercises

Norway's Olympic skiers practice balance exercises daily. Here are a few exercises to help you with your balance. The first two exercises work on static balance — balance which does not move laterally. The third drill and the skating drills deal with dynamic balance.

Start with one-leg balance exercises. Balance on one foot then the other. Hold the balance on each foot as long as possible. Time yourself on how long you can hold each balanced position. The muscles on the inside and the outside of your hips and thighs both work in this drill. As you start to sway outward, the inside muscles contract. As you start to sway inward, the outside muscles contract.

Balancing on a flexed leg is a bit more difficult. Take your one-foot balance position. Slowly lower your hips until your knee is at about a 60-degree angle. Your hips should be eight to 10 inches lower than in a normal standing position. Move up and down for 15 seconds, or until you have lost your balance. Now do it on the other leg. The same muscles work as in the previous drill, but because you are moving up and down, other muscles come into play and the muscles which hold you balanced must react to different stimuli.

Hopping balance is a more advanced drill. With your weight balanced on one foot, hold for five seconds or until you start to lose your balance then hop to the other foot and hold. Continue hopping from one leg to the other. Learn to hold each new balanced position for five seconds. Start with 6-inch hops. Eventually aim for 24-inch hops.

In this drill, the muscles in your legs, which control balance, work as well as the muscles in your hips. If you don't hop far enough outward, the muscles on the outside of your hips must work to pull you into the proper position. If you shift too much weight outward, the inner thigh muscles must pull you back or you will fall outward. This drill is critical to teaching your brain just how quickly it must shift the body weight and how far it can shift it.

Balance Problem Causes

If you have trouble balancing, it might be caused by vision problems, inner ear problems, or problems with the cerebellum, a part of the brain that is in the rear of the brain. To check whether it is your eyes or ears, go to ophthalmologist or optician and to a doctor who specializes in inner ear measurements. Not all ear-nose-throat specialists have the equipment necessary to measure whether the crystals in the inner ear are free-floating. Cerebellum problems are more difficult to deal with, but balance exercises may improve its ability to help you to balance

Summer Skating and Skiing

Both balance and conditioning are necessary for everybody—and essential for cross country skiers. Inline roller skates, with or without poles, and roller skis are ideal conditioning for both. In Norway, as soon as the snow leaves the ground, roller skis emerge. Young and old, beginners and Olympians all can be seen rolling up and down the hills. The world's best female skier roller skis past my house most days when the roads are clear of snow.

Dynamic Balance

Roller blades or in-line roller skates as well as roller skis will help you with the dynamic balance needed on the snow. Skiing on in-line skates can be quite easy, especially for skilled skiers. Think about it; you don't have six feet of ski attached to your feet so the skates are quite easy to turn. The pavement is usually smooth and consistent, and the whole situation is really quite predictable. The skates also hold the road easier than skis hold the snow.

If you are comfortable going left and right while roller skating, start being creative and do some things which will increase your balance on skis. Set up a slalom course. Use rocks, traffic cones, or your kids' toys, to make a course that you can skate through — just like in the Olympic slalom course. Stagger the "gates," create a course which will challenge our balance — then start skating. Cut left and right, wide turns and sharp turns. Make it fun. It will help you to be a better skater and a better skier.

Setting gates on a moderately steep road is also a great training aid. It simulates the movements of skiing and can help you to develop an aggressive attitude. Set them with lots of turns — short turns, then try to generate speed between the gates. Don't try to improve your technique. Instead, try to acquire that attitude of aggressively going after the next turn rather than waiting for it to come to you. If you can do it on skates, you'll be able to do it on skis.

Play on skates while you increase your sense of balance and equilibrium. It's still important to make some turns, but the emphasis should be toward doing things on skates that allow you to move free from the preoccupation of technique. Learn how to move for balance, not for looks! Also, don't worry about strength or endurance or anaerobic capacity — just make it fun. If you put some chutzpa into the games you play on skates, you'll get stronger, and you'll have more fun in the process.

Ice skating is another balance activity which you may want to try. For the national ski team in Norway, we bring in the Olympic skating coach to help us with skating technique and balance.

Effective conditioning helps your body to be the best tool that it can be for effective skiing. It also keeps your physiological age reduced. A well-conditioned 60-year-old may have the musculature and heart of a person less than 30. So, effective conditioning can make you look and feel better. And certainly, it will reduce any unwanted tiredness or soreness on your

CHAPTER 12
Skiing with kids

Helping children enjoy skiing, and making it a "fun" activity, is something that we all should strive for. It is important to go skiing on the children's premises. The parents or adults skiing with the kids have to make sure to wear enough clothes so that we can play with the kids in their tempo. Make sure the kids also keep warm, but the balance is hard – it is important that they do not wear too many clothes as.

The first skiing activities with our kids was in our yard, when the first snow had fallen. We could still see the grass. We first practice with the kids standing between our skis, gliding down the hills. This gave them the feel of gliding and speed. And we had to do it over and over again. The children walked on their skis back up the hill or we carried them on our shoulders when they got tired. After practicing skiing with the kids they wanted to try on their own. They wanted to use poles, but we encouraged them to try skiing without the poles. Skiing without poles would help their balance and usually the poles cause irritation and interfere with their skiing at first. It helps that the parents also ski without poles, this also makes it easier to help the children up on their skis again after falling – because they **will** fall.

    The children enjoy skiing and feel the glide and speed. Here are one video of the children skiing with us when they were two and a half years old

    When the kids get the feel of gliding you can try skiing you can try going for a hike. Set a goal for the skiing activity. At first we skied only a few hundred meters, but we packed lunch and had the kids agree on the goal, where we would eat our lunch. The kids get motivated by having a common goal and the knowledge of the treats they would get when they got there. At our stop the kids can explore the area with and without skis on, while we prepare the lunch.

When the children are small and not able to ski by themselves, we have to bring the pulk/carrier. It is however smart to bring the pulk along as the children get bigger, because they do get tired and would like to relax for parts of the hike.

Make it fun to ski. Let the kids do what motivates them, like playing with water in the yard. The important thing is that the children get the feel of skiing and have fun at the same time. Some times it is easier to focus, but not always.

Here is a picture of the kids playing in the yard of their grandparents, having a great time on their own premises.

Children think differently than adults, so it is important to listen to them in order to make it fun for them to ski. As adults we want to learn how to ski right, doing the techniques and going fast. But for kids, at least when they are young, the most important thing is to have fun and play. Maybe we adults have something to learn from the children?! I filmed Ella playing "hide and seek" in her grandparents' yard.

Here are some videos of kids skiing and playing on skis:

Links for e-book	Url- address for printed book
Press on the link (ctrl + click)	**Write address into your web-browser**
Going downhill one skiing, one in pulk	https://vimeo.com/300127174/37a788700d
Skiing inside the house	https://vimeo.com/312205048/f646cdf534
Playing hide and seek with skis on	https://vimeo.com/300142166/77d2bea5e3
Andrea skiing in the mountains	https://vimeo.com/312204744/50d4e139ee

<u>Playing hide and seek with skis on</u>

It is not important to ski the longest or to have a perfect technique, even though good technique also helps enjoying skiing as an activity. In my family we have always build jumps and tracks with bumps in them to work on our abilities on skis. It is important that the grownups play with the kids. It is even more fun skiing when mom, dad or grandparents fall while playing or going down a hill.

Play games with the kids and have fun with skis on your feet. In my family we have a fun-race with games for children and adults every easter. The task is to go to the different posts to answer questions (like Jaopardy), ski down a hill with obstacles or throw rings, like in the photo. Everybody gets prizes and everybody participates.

Picture to the left:
A modern pulk/karrier with two kids
pulled through the forest

Picture to the right (above):
Happy and sleeping kids in their pulk
during a skitrip

Games for the whole family at Easter

Links for e-book	Url- address for printed book
▐█▌🎥	
Press on the link (ctrl + click)	**Write address into your web-browser**
Ella going downhill alone	https://vimeo.com/312204953/e56a8f7e9d
Even going downhill	https://vimeo.com/312204780/9b3f053ce0
Skiing home from Tryvann	https://vimeo.com/300129095/80f2f8fa44
Happy skier	https://vimeo.com/311045444/aadd93a42d

Outside the big and small towns in Norway there are places in the forest you can ski to and buy a snack (or a full meal if you want). People can also walk and bike to these diners as well. The goal of getting to a diner has motivated our kids to ski as they get older. There we have a hot chocolate and something to eat. It makes it even easier to go skiing because the adults do not need to pack food and drinks. And the kids are excited to get different treats they do not get at home.

As the children get older they can ski longer, but do not forget to have a common goal for the ski(trip/tour). Always make room for whatever technique or the funny walk that will present itself.

EPILOGUE

We have tried to portray the basic principles for Nordic skiing. But remember that each person is a little different. Your skiing will be unique to you. Your technique, just as every other skier from beginner to world champion, will change according to the type of snow, the angle of the slope, speed and level of fatigue. There is no one way to ski —just some basic principles.

And as with any other activity in life, the more you do it, the better you get at it and the more fun it becomes.

So condition yourself, practice your techniques, and ski a lot. And as we say in Norway, *"God tur"* Have a good tour — through the forests and through your life!

Index

U

understanding muscles, *4, 131, 167–168*

W

waxable skis, *94, 119, 167–168*
waxing, *4–5, 14, 22, 24, 86, 105–107, 109, 112, 114–117, 167–168*
waxless skis, *4, 12, 84, 94, 118–119, 167–168*
wedge, *2–3, 46, 48, 51, 54–57, 60–62, 64, 149, 163, 165, 167–168*
wedge turn, *3, 56–57, 61, 167–168*

Y

you, *2, 5–12, 14–18, 20, 22–25, 27–46, 48–55, 57–70, 72–75, 79–86, 88–107, 109–112, 114–116, 118, 121–130, 133, 136–153, 155, 160–161, 167–168*

Z

zero skis, *118–119, 167–168*

Made in the USA
Columbia, SC
08 November 2020